DISCRIMINATION
IN
LABOR MARKETS

DISCRIMINATION
IN
LABOR MARKETS

edited by

Orley Ashenfelter and Albert Rees

PRINCETON UNIVERSITY PRESS

PRINCETON, NEW JERSEY

All Rights Reserved
LCC: 72-4037
ISBN: 0-691-04170-9

This book has been composed in Linotype Caledonia

Printed in the United States of America
by Princeton University Press, Princeton, New Jersey

Library of Congress Cataloging in
Publication data appears on the last printed
page of this book.

CONTENTS

CONTRIBUTORS

KENNETH ARROW is Professor of Economics, Harvard University.

ORLEY ASHENFELTER is Professor of Economics and Director of the Industrial Relations Section, Princeton University.

BARBARA R. BERGMANN is Professor of Economics, University of Maryland.

RICHARD FREEMAN is Associate Professor of Economics, Harvard University.

DALE L. HIESTAND is Professor of Business and Senior Research Associate, Conservation of Human Resources, Columbia University.

HERBERT HILL is National Labor Director of the N.A.A.C.P. and lectures at Princeton University and the New School for Social Research.

RONALD OAXACA is Assistant Professor of Economics, University of Massachusetts.

MELVIN W. REDER is Professor of Economics, Graduate Center, City University of New York and Senior Research Associate, National Bureau of Economic Research.

PHYLLIS A. WALLACE is Visiting Professor, Massachusetts Institute of Technology.

FINIS WELCH is Professor of Economics, University of California at Los Angeles.

INTRODUCTION

This book contains the papers presented at a Princeton University Conference on Discrimination in Labor Markets held on October 7 and 8, 1971, and sponsored by the Industrial Relations Section and the Woodrow Wilson School of Public and International Affairs.

Discrimination in wages by race and sex is a topic that has long interested economists, but thorough theoretical and quantitative analysis of it is rather recent. The beginning of this thorough analysis can best be dated by the publication of Gary S. Becker's *Economics of Discrimination* (University of Chicago Press, 1957). When one considers the quality of the analysis and the importance of the topic, this work attracted surprisingly little attention. In the first nine years after publication, it sold fewer than 2,000 copies.[1]

More recently, scientific interest in discrimination in labor markets has increased markedly. The rise of first the civil rights and later the women's liberation movements, the passage of the Civil Rights Act, and the creation of the Equal Employment Opportunity Commission have stimulated new scholarly studies. The opening of new and relevant data bases has helped to sustain this interest; the most important of these is the 1967 Survey of Economic Opportunity, which is the source of data for several of the papers in this volume.

By 1971, enough work on the topic was in progress at different universities and other institutions to warrant bringing together the researchers in the field so that they could discuss and criticize one another's work. As plans for the

[1] See A. J. Morin, "The Market for Professional Writing in Economics," *American Economic Review*, 56, No. 5 (May 1966), 406-407.

conference were made, it also seemed desirable to have nonacademic participants—men and women with practical experience in business, government, trade unions, and civil rights organizations. We felt that the comments of such people could improve the final versions of the papers, that they could learn from the research, and that their presence would induce the academic economists to state their findings in a form intelligible to a wider audience. As is often the case at a conference with diverse participants, the discussion was always lively and occasionally acrimonious, but it is our feeling that the original purposes were well achieved. This volume contains the revised versions of the papers presented in October 1971 and the formal discussion of them. We have not felt it possible to summarize the wide-ranging informal discussions that followed.

The papers begin with Kenneth Arrow's elucidation of the theoretical foundations of the economic analysis of discrimination in labor markets. As Melvin Reder remarks in his discussion of Arrow's paper, this topic is important to economists primarily because it provides a solid, logical foundation to their applied work and its applications to public policy. Arrow begins with a clear and concise discussion of the impact on wages in the labor market of racial or other preferences by employers and by the majority of workers. Although this analysis provides a rigorous and plausible economic explanation for the existence of differential wage payments between different groups in the short run, it runs into difficulties in analyses of long-run wage differentials in competitive markets.

Because of this difficulty, Arrow investigates two possible explanations for the existence of discriminatory wage differentials in the longer run. The first explanation stresses costs of adjustment to a new equilibrium in response to a disequilibrating force, while the second considers the possibility that the basic cause of the discriminatory differentials is the imperfect information of employers rather than specific racial preferences.

In the second paper, Finis Welch turns to the relationship between schooling and labor market discrimination. He begins by presenting new evidence on the comparison of the economic benefits from schooling for black and white workers using large bodies of cross-sectional data for 1959 and 1966. Welch examines the change in the returns to a year of schooling for both black and white workers over this period and concludes that there has been a significant increase in the rate of return to schooling for black workers relative to white workers. He suggests several explanations for this phenomenon and argues in detail that increases in the relative quality of the schooling of black youngsters over the last five or six decades may be an important element in the explanation.

Since many policies designed to affect discrimination deal with changes in the institutional environment of labor markets, it is important to obtain *empirical* evidence on the extent to which the presence of various institutions tends to mitigate or intensify the racial and other preferences that cause discrimination. Orley Ashenfelter's paper presents a method for estimating the effect of the presence of the institution of trade unionism on the wages of black workers relative to whites and the wages of female workers relative to males. The paper also discusses the factors likely to determine a union's policy on racial issues. Ashenfelter's arguments suggest that craft unions are likely to be more discriminatory than industrial unions. His empirical results support this argument. They suggest that industrial unions may have raised, while craft unions may have reduced, the average wage of black workers relative to white workers, where the basis of comparison in both cases is nonunion labor markets.

In recent years public discussion of discrimination against women in the labor market has increased substantially. Ronald Oaxaca's paper provides a framework for measuring the extent of discrimination against women and an application of the proposed method to data from the

Survey of Economic Opportunity. Oaxaca pays special attention to the problem of measuring factors associated with differences in the productivity of male and female workers in the labor market, concentrating on differences in the amount of labor-market experience that workers have. His results suggest that a large component of the observed male/female wage differential remains unexplained even after adjustment for measurable productivity factors.

In the final paper Phyllis Wallace examines public policy toward discrimination against black and female workers. Her paper describes the legal mechanisms available for taking steps against discrimination and how these legal mechanisms have been translated into operating policies since their enactment. The diversity of both legal remedies and agencies involved in the equal employment opportunity process makes it difficult to assess the actual effects of government influence. However, Wallace uses the limited experience available to examine alternative strategies for public policy in this area.

The treatment of discrimination in labor markets in this volume is by no means complete. For example, there is no discussion of discrimination against Spanish-speaking workers, Orientals, and native Americans, an area where economic research has been hampered by lack of data. In addition, there are no papers that attempt to measure the effects of government policy—an area in which some work has been done, but more is necessary. It is our hope that some of these gaps will be filled in the near future and that this volume will be helpful to those who undertake to fill them.

Orley Ashenfelter
Albert Rees

DISCRIMINATION
IN
LABOR MARKETS

Kenneth J. Arrow

THE THEORY OF DISCRIMINATION

1. INTRODUCTION

The fact that different groups of workers, be they skilled or unskilled, black or white, male or female, receive different wages, invites the explanation that the different groups must differ according to some characteristic valued on the market. In standard economic theory, we think first of differences in productivity. The notion of discrimination involves the additional concept that personal characteristics of the worker unrelated to productivity are also valued on the market. Such personal characteristics as race, ethnic background, and sex have been frequently adduced in this context.

Discrimination in this paper is considered only as it appears on the market. Obviously, one can have discrimination in the same sense whenever decisions are made that concern other individuals, namely, when personal characteristics other than those properly relevant enter into the decision. Deliberate racial segregation and discrimination in entrance to schools and colleges, deprivation of the right to vote along social and sexual lines, and discriminatory taxation are all examples of nonmarket discrimination.

It may as well be admitted that the term "discrimination" has value implications that can never be completely eradicated, though they can be sterilized for specific empirical and descriptive analyses. I have spoken of personal characteristics that are "unrelated to productivity" and not "properly relevant." These terms imply definitions of product and of relevancy which are themselves value judgments or at any rate decisions by the scholar. The black steel worker may be thought of as producing blackness as well as steel, both evaluated in the market. We are singling out the former as a special subject for analysis because somehow we think it appropriate for the steel industry to produce steel and not for it to produce a black or white work force.

However, the value judgments are intrinsic only in determining which wage differences we regard as worth studying as an example of discrimination, *not* in the empirical or theoretical analysis of any form of discrimination once specified.

In the following, I will address myself specifically to racial discrimination in the labor market. For the most part, the analysis extends with no difficulty to sexual discrimination. The other markets in which discrimination has been most observed, especially housing but also insurance and capital, are analyzed by the same general methods, but the operation of these markets has led more often to simple exclusion and less to price differentials.

The basic aim here is to use as far as possible neoclassical tools in the analysis of discrimination. As will be seen, even though the basic neoclassical assumptions of utility and profit-maximization are always retained, many of the usual assumptions will be relaxed at one point or another: convexity of indifference surfaces, costless adjustment, perfect information, perfect capital markets. As I will try to show, the abandonment of each of these assumptions is motivated by a clearly compelling reason in the theoretical structure of the subject. Personally, I believe there are many other economic phenomena whose explanation entails the abandonment of each of these assumptions, so the steps proposed here are not ad hoc analyses but should be important elements in a more general theory capable of analyzing the effects of social factors on economic behavior without either lumping them into an uninformative category of "imperfections" or jumping to a precipitate rejection of neoclassical theory with all its analytic power.

4

The first application of neoclassical theory to discrimination that I know of is that of Edgeworth, but the main study to date has been that of Becker.[1] The analysis to be presented here appears in a more technical form in an earlier paper.[2] It seeks to develop further Becker's models and to relate them more closely to the theory of general competitive equilibrium, though frequently by way of contrast rather than agreement.

Since I am presenting here the theory of discrimination in the labor market and not the entire theory of racial differences in income, I abstract from differences in productivity between the groups of workers. In an empirical study, it will be necessary to allow for this possibility. In the case of blacks and whites, some possible causes of productivity differences have been established (differences in educational quantity and quality, family size and socio-economic status, and household headed by woman); and others surmised (culturally varying attitudes toward work and future-orientation derived from the heritage of slavery and other historical factors).[3] These differences themselves may

[1] See for example, F. Y. Edgeworth, "Equal Pay to Men and Women for Equal Work," *Economic Journal*, 31 (1922), 431-457; and Gary Becker, *The Economics of Discrimination* (Chicago: University of Chicago Press, 1959).

[2] For further analysis see Kenneth J. Arrow, "Models of Job Discrimination," Chapter 2 in A. H. Pascal (ed.) *Racial Discrimination in Economic Life* (Lexington, Mass.: D. C. Heath, 1972) pp. 83-102; and Arrow, "Some Models of Race in the Labor Market," Chapter 6 in A. H. Pascal, *ibid.*

[3] See for example, O. D. Duncan, "Inheritance of Poverty or Inheritance of Race?" in D. P. Moynihan (ed.) *On Understanding Poverty* (New York: Basic Books, 1969), Ch. 4, pp. 85-110. Although my concern here is with discrimination and not with productivity differences, I must note my skepticism about the frequently made argument that blacks have less future-orientation. For this disregards the well-known fact that at any given income level blacks save at least as much as whites. This remains essentially true even when "income" is understood to mean "permanent income"; see Milton Friedman, *The Theory of the Consumption Function* (Princeton, N.J.: Princeton University Press, 1957), pp. 79-85; and H. W. Mooney and L. R. Klein,

be the result of discrimination in other areas of life. But for theoretical analysis of discrimination in the labor market, it is legitimate to assume that there are two groups of workers, to be denoted by B and W, which are perfect substitutes in production.

For the simplest model, then, we have a large number of firms all producing the same product with the same production function. Discrimination means that some economic agent has some negative valuation for B or positive valuation for W, or both, a valuation for which the agent both is willing to pay and has the opportunity to pay. The agents who could possibly discriminate are the employer, who might sacrifice profits to reduce or eliminate B employment in his plant, or the W workers who might accept a lower wage to work in a plant with more W and less B workers. (It is also possible that, for products sold on a face-to-face basis, customers might discriminate by being willing to pay higher prices to buy from whites; this case could be studied along similar lines but will not be dealt with here.) Not all discriminatory feelings can find expression in the market; an entrepreneur who has a distaste for competing against firms with B workers has no way, within the economic system at least, of expressing his tastes and therefore of influencing wage levels.

I assume that, given the tastes, the markets work smoothly. General equilibrium requires full employment of both B and W workers; the wages of both will adjust to clear the market, and the discriminatory tastes will be reflected in wage differences.

Let us first consider the simplest case, that in which the employer discriminates. Then he accepts a trade-off between profits, π, and the numbers of B and W employees. That is, we suppose he seeks to maximize, not profits, but a utility function, $U(\pi, B, W)$. We assume, to get the sim-

"Negro-white Savings Differentials and the Consumption Function Problem," *Econometrica*, 21 (1953), 425-456.

6

plest case, that there is only one type of labor; in the short run, we also take capital as given, so that output is $f(W+B)$, since the two kinds of labor are perfect substitutes (at a one-to-one ratio). If we take output as numeraire, then profits are given by the expression

$$(1) \qquad \pi = f(W+B) - w_W W - w_B B,$$

where w_W and w_B are the wage rates, taken as given by the employers. If we proceed along conventional lines, the employer equates the marginal productivity of each hand of labor to the price to him. But here the "price" of B labor is the market price, w_B, *plus* the price the employer is willing to pay, in terms of profits, for reducing his B labor force by one. This second term is what Becker has termed the "discrimination coefficient," to be designated as d_B; it is the negative of the marginal rate of substitution of profits for B labor. If, as we usually suppose, the marginal utility of B labor is negative, then the discrimination coefficient, d_B, is positive.

In symbols,

$$(2) \qquad MP_B = w_B + d_B,$$

where $d_B = - MR_{\pi,B}$. Similarly,

$$(3) \qquad MP_W = w_W + d_W,$$

where d_W is negative (or zero if the employer has no positive liking for having W workers). But we are assuming that the two types of labor are interchangeable in production, so that $MP_W = MP_B = MP_L$, say. Then, from (2) and (3), $w_W + d_{dW} = w_B + d_B$, or

$$(4) \qquad w_W - w_B = d_B - d_W > 0,$$

so that equilibrium requires that W wages exceed B wages, as might be expected.

For the moment, assume that all firms have the same utility function, $U(\pi, B, W,)$. It then appears reasonable to assume that all hire the same amounts of B and W (but we will return to this point in the next section). Then each firm's labor force is the same, and the allocation of labor is efficient. The effects of discrimination are purely distributive. The most obvious implication then is that B workers are paid less than their marginal product, so that the W workers and employers together gain. Also, the W workers clearly gain, or at least do not lose, from (3), with $d_W \leq 0$. The effect on profits, however, depends on the exact nature of the utility function. Under the assumption made, it follows from (1-3) and the fact that $MP_W = MP_B = MP_L$ that,

$$(5) \qquad \pi = f(L) - (MP_L)L + d_W W + d_B B,$$

where $L = W + B$, the total labor force of the firm. If there were no discrimination, profits would be,

$$\pi_0 = f(L) - (MP_L)L,$$

and therefore the change in profits is simply,

$$(6) \qquad \pi - \pi_0 = d_W W + d_B B.$$

The right-hand term has a simple interpretation. If we consider an increase in the firm's labor force with the proportions of W and B workers constant, then the negative of the marginal rate of substitution of profits for this balanced increase is simply $d_W (W/L) + d_B (B/L)$; this is the firm's need for additional profits to compensate it for a balanced increase in size. This term may of course be positive or negative.

However, a plausible hypothesis which we shall maintain hereafter is that employers' satisfactions depend only on the ratio of B to W workers. In that case,

$$(7) \qquad d_W W + d_B B = 0,$$

and (6) tells us that employers neither gain nor lose by their discriminatory behavior. The entire effect is that of a transfer from B to W workers.

Let us now relax the assumption that utility functions are identical among firms. We continue to assume that for each firm, the utility depends only on the ratio of W to B workers, but some firms may be more discriminatory than others, in the sense that the marginal rate of substitution of profits for B workers will be more negative at any given ratio, B/W. Equations (4) and (7) hold for each firm, at least each firm that employs both types of workers. They can be regarded as a pair of linear equations in d_W and d_B, to yield,

$$d_B = W(w_W - w_B)/(W + B),$$
$$d_W = -B(w_W - w_B)/(W + B),$$

which can be rewritten,

$$W/L = d_B/(w_W - w_B);$$
$$B/L = -d_W/(w_W - w_B).$$

Since $d_B > 0$, if there are both B and W workers, it must be that $w_W > w_B$, as before. We will observe firms with different ratios of W to L. The firms that display the most discrimination at the margin, i.e. the highest values of d_B, have the highest ratios of W to L. Thus an observation on all the firms in existence at equilibrium will reveal a dispersion of W-proportions in the labor force, and these ratios will measure the varying degrees of discrimination. Thus a partial degree of segregation appears; the B workers tend to be found in the less discriminatory firms, the W workers in the more discriminatory ones.

However, further analysis leads to implications which might raise some empirical questions. Specifically, equation (2) still holds, with $MP_B = MP_L$. Hence, according to the model, MP_L is higher for more discriminating firms. But then if we assume diminishing marginal productivity of labor, it follows that, the less discriminatory the firm, the larger it will be. This accords with common sense; discrimination is costly to the entrepreneur and acts as a tax on him, since it shifts his demand for labor to the more costly component. Hence, it restricts his scale.

Since MP_L is no longer the same from firm to firm, it follows that production is no longer efficient. The previous strong statements about the incidence of discrimination no longer hold exactly either. However, their general thrust is still probably correct. Efficiency losses are not apt to be great, and the main redistribution is still likely to be from B workers to W workers.

It has been seen that competition tends to reduce the degree of discrimination in the market, in the sense that the unweighted average of discrimination coefficients of the different firms exceeds the average weighted in proportion to the number of workers.

This result, which may or may not be empirically reasonable, appears more strongly and less likely when one pushes the analysis into the long run. Now we are assuming that capital, which has been hitherto held fixed, is adjusted optimally to the size of the labor force. Then capital will flow to the more profitable enterprises which, in this context, are the less discriminatory. In the long run, output is therefore simply proportional to labor (assuming the production function displays constant returns to capital and labor). The marginal product of labor is then constant. As a result, the competitive effect just studied assumes an exaggerated form. Only the least discriminatory firms survive. Indeed, if there were any firms which did not discriminate at all, these would be the only ones to survive the competitive struggle. Since in fact racial discrimination has survived for a long time, we must assume that the model just presented must have some limitation to which we will return in Section 4.

We have dealt extensively with the assumption of discrimination by employers. But, as we observed earlier, discrimination by co-workers is also a possibility. The most straightforward extension of the preceding analysis is to the case of complementary services. Suppose now there are two kinds of workers, say foremen and floor workers. It is the foremen who like working with W's and dislike working with B's. As before, we assume that the likes or dislikes are governed by the ratio of W to B floor workers. Each foreman then chooses among alternative employment opportunities on the basis of both wages and the W/B ratio. Assume that all foremen have the same utility function.

The equilibrium in this model is a trifle unorthodox. Instead of an equilibrium wage for foremen, there is an equilibrium relation between foremen's wages and W/B ratios in firms. Every firm must lie on this curve, and the equilibrium curve will be one of the foremen's indifference curves between wages and W/B.

Let F be the number of foremen, and w_F their wage. Then the firm faces fixed w_W and w_B for the floor workers and a fixed *relation*,

$$(8) \qquad w_F = w_F(W/L)$$

where $L = W + B$ is the total floor force. The firm's short-run profits are defined by,

$$(9) \qquad \pi = f(L, F) - w_W W - w_B B - w_F F,$$

where it is assumed, as before, that W and B floor workers are perfect substitutes.

Assume now that firms have no discriminatory tastes. They seek only to maximize profits. They will still not hire B workers at equal wages with W since an increase in W decreases the wages and therefore the cost of F, while an increase in B increases the cost of F. Hence, a W worker is worth more than his marginal product, while a B worker is worth less, exactly as in the case of employer discrimination. Further, the extent of the premiums over or deficits from marginal product depends only on the ratio of W to B. Hence, the previous analysis applies with suitable modifications. W workers are paid more than their marginal product, B workers less. If all firms wind up with the same levels of W and B, then the results are entirely parallel to those for employer discrimination: production remains efficient, and the entire incidence of the foremen's discrimination falls negatively on the B workers and positively to an equal extent on the W workers.

As in the case of employer discrimination, the extent of the wage difference between B and W workers depends on the extent of discrimination. The precise formula is of some interest. Recall that, by (8), w_F is a function of the ratio, W/L. By w'_F, I will mean the derivative of w_F with respect to this ratio (this is negative). Then w'_F/w_F is the proportional rate of change of the demanded wage rate (along the equilibrium indifference curve between foremen's wages and W proportion in the floor force) and therefore is a measure of discriminatory tastes. Let S_F be total payments to foremen, S_L total payments to floor workers. Then the following has been shown:[4]

$$(10) \qquad \frac{w_W - w_B}{MP_L} = - \frac{w'_F}{w_F} \frac{S_F}{S_L}$$

The left-hand side is the market wage differential due to discriminatory tastes of foremen relative to the wage level in the absence of discrimination.

This formula has an interesting aspect. Given the degree of discrimination as measured by $- w'_F/w_F$, the observed wage differential depends on the ratio S_F/S_L. That is, the more important the share of foremen in the output of the firm relative to floor laborers, the greater the wage differential.

The language of the preceding analysis has assumed that it is the foremen or other supervisory employees who discriminate according to the composition of the floor workers. But the analysis itself is completely abstract. It may be illuminating to reverse the roles. Suppose that production workers have strong discriminatory feelings about their supervisors. Certainly the idea that white workers strongly resent being bossed by black supervisors or male workers by female foremen (foreladies? forepersons?) is a common one. Then if in (10) we understand by W and B those kinds of supervisory workers, by L the total number of such

[4] Arrow, "Some Models of Race in the Labor Market," Section B.

workers, and by F the floor workers, we have an excellent explanation of discrimination against B supervisory workers, for S_F then would be very large indeed compared with S_L.

Foremen may possibly differ in their tastes for discrimination. One might suppose that this will lead to a reduction in market wage differentials, analogous to the situation with employer discrimination. But a fuller analysis of this case remains to be done.

2. NONCONVEXITIES IN INDIFFERENCE SURFACES AND OPPORTUNITIES

I have gradually become convinced that the usual assumption that indifference surfaces are convex is inapplicable to the case of racial discrimination and indeed to many other problems in the economics of externalities. Pollution provides another example; Starrett has already pointed to the importance of nonconvexity in this context.[5] Assumptions which seem very reasonable in the contexts of discriminatory behavior *necessarily* imply a nonconvexity of the indifference surfaces of the firms in the case of employer discrimination or of the firm's profit function in the case of discrimination by complementary workers.

Actually, my view is that nonconvexity of indifference surfaces is in fact a widespread phenomenon. An excellent example in commodities with no externalities is residential location. One *could* after all live half the time in one place and half in the other. Convexity implies that such an arrangement would be at least as good as the least preferred of the two locations. If one is indifferent to the two, then one will prefer the mixture. In fact, taken literally, convexity would imply that individuals would be willing to spend half of any minute in one place and half in the other.

[5] See D. Starrett, "Fundamental Non-convexities in the Theory of Externalities," *Journal of Economic Theory*, 4 (1972), 180-199.

But (except for a few "beautiful people") most individuals find it preferable to live in one place, even though there may be another to which they are indifferent.

Indeed, if one looks through the literature, it is hard to find a convincing intuitive explanation of convexity of indifference surfaces. The best argument is that convexity is a necessary and sufficient condition for the continuity of demand functions. But this argument applies only to individual demand functions. Since each individual is small on the scale of the entire market, even the largest discontinuity in an individual demand function implies a negligible discontinuity in the market demand function. Hence, observations which suggest approximate continuity in market demand functions in no way imply convexity of indifference surfaces. In particular, the existence of general competitive equilibrium remains unaffected, or, to be precise, the existence of an approximate equilibrium of supply and demand on all markets can be demonstrated. (This line of argument was suggested initially by Farrell and subsequently developed by Bator, Rothenberg, Aumann, and Starr; for one exposition, see Arrow and Hahn.)[6]

It is true that the market demand function, if it is effectively continuous, can be derived by adding up a new set of individual demand functions, each derived from a "convexified" indifference map obtained from the original by filling in all the holes in the indifference surfaces. From the point of view of prices and total market quantities, the new-

---

[6] For further analysis, see M. J. Farrell, "The Convexity Assumption in the Theory of Competitive Markets," *Journal of Political Economy*, 67 (1969), 377-379; Francis Bator, "Convexity, Efficiency, and Markets," *Journal of Political Economy*, 69 (1961), 480-483; Jerome Rothenberg, "Non-convexity, Aggregation, and Pareto Optimality," *Journal of Political Economy*, 68 (1960), 435-468; R. J. Aumann, "Existence of Competitive Equilibria in Markets with a Continuum of Traders," *Econometrica*, 34 (1966), 1-17; R. Starr, "Quasi-equilibria in Markets with Nonconvex Preferences," *Econometrica*, 37 (1969), 25-38; and Kenneth J. Arrow and Frank Hahn, *General Competitive Analysis* (San Francisco: Holden-Day, 1971), Ch. 7.

ly formed indifference map predicts as well as does the original, and therefore one might be tempted to assume that one could act "as if" indifference surfaces were convex, though with some flat surfaces. But there is a loss of information, for the *distribution* of goods among individuals is quite different from what it would be if all individuals had convex indifference surfaces. Thus, in our residential location example, the market totals (how many people-hours are spent in each place) and the rents in the two places are well predicted by the convex approximation. But recognizing the underlying nonconvexities enables us to predict that half the people will be in one place all the time and half in the other, instead of each individual's spending half his time in one place and half in the other.

Let me give a brief diagrammatic illustration. Suppose every individual has the same indifference map, as given by Figure 1, and the same initial endowment, represented by A. One's initial reaction, conditioned by years of working

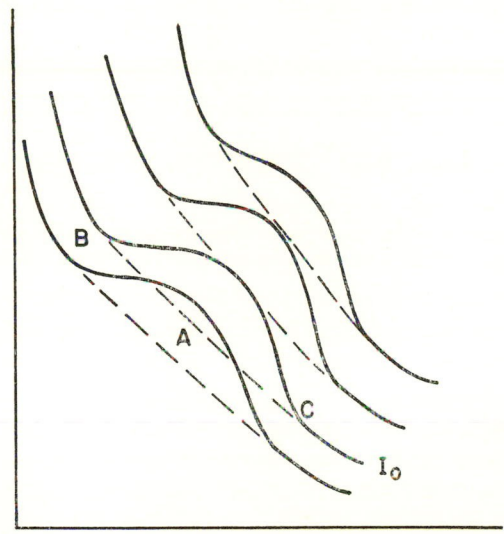

FIGURE 1

15

with convex indifference maps, is to assume that there is no trade; since all individuals are alike in every economic respect, they should wind up alike, which in this case means each with his own initial bundle. But this is clearly false. In fact the equilibrium can be obtained as follows: convexify each indifference curve by filling in the hole with a straight line segment tangent to the curve at both ends, as, for example, the segment BC on curve I_0. Now we see that, if we pretend for the moment that the convexified map is the true indifference map for each individual, then each individual winds up on the convexified curve I_0. Since this curve is flat at the point A, the price ratio is determined by the slope of BC. Now return to the individual, who has the original indifference curve I_0. At these prices, he will maximize utility at two different points, B and C, but not at any point in between. If, for example, A is half-way between B and C, then market equilibrium is realized by having half the individuals at B and half at C. If A is two-thirds of the way from B to C, the market equilibrium is realized by having two-thirds of the individuals buy the bundle C and one-third the bundle B. Note that each individual is at a point of maximum utility for him subject to his budget constraint, so that this is truly a competitive equilibrium and therefore efficient. (The earlier reference to "approximate equilibrium" is relevant when there are not enough individuals to split them in the right proportions between B and C. Thus, if A is .71 of the way from B to C and there are only 50 individuals in the economy, there should be 35½ individuals at C and 14½ at B. Thus, at C or B the discrepancy between supply and demand cannot be reduced below half an individual. This is a relatively minor discrepancy between supply and demand.)

Thus nonconvexity implies the existence of distinct *niches* for economic agents in a sense of the word which I take to be close to that used in ecology. One observes agents, identical in their economic data, engaged in diverse consumption patterns or other economic activities. Any given agent may be indifferent between several of these niches, but equilibrium requires their coexistence. This argument underlies Adam Smith's discussion of specialization as opposed to Ricardo's, which was based on differences in the productivities of individuals or nations; it has been made explicit in an important but neglected paper of Houthakker.[7]

Let me now apply these abstract concepts to racial discrimination. We take up a model due to Becker and in a different form to Welch and not analyzed above.[8] Now we locate the discriminatory tastes in the W workers who are perfect substitutes for the B workers. To keep matters as simple as possible, assume there is only one kind of labor. Then, analogous to the assumption made about complementary forms of labor, we now assume that W workers have an indifference map between wages and the proportion W, so that at equilibrium, there is a relation,

$$(11) \qquad w_W = w_W(W/L),$$

where w_W decreases as W/L increases from 0 to 1. As part of profit maximization, the firm will certainly seek that combination of W and B which will minimize the cost of hiring whatever total number of workers, $W + B = L$, it does hire. This cost is

$$(12) \qquad C(W, B) = w_W(W/L) W + w_B B.$$

But it is easy to see that a firm will always achieve minimum cost with either an all-W or an all-B labor force. The two might be equally cheap, but certainly any combination with W and B both positive will be more costly than at least one extreme case and possibly more costly than both. To see this, consider two cases:

[7] See Hendrick S. Houthakker, "Economics and Biology: Specialization and Speciation," *Kyklos*, 9 (1956), 181-187.

[8] See for example, Gary Becker, *op. cit.*; and Finis Welch, "Labor Market Discrimination: An Interpretation of Income Differences in the Rural South," *Journal of Political Economy*, 75 (1967), 225-240.

17

(a) $w_W(1) \geqq w_B$: Recall that $W/L = 1$ means an all-W labor force. Then for any W, $0 < W < L$, $w_W(W/L) > w_W(1) \geqq w_B$, and therefore $w_W(W/L)W + w_BB > w_B (W+B) = w_BL$; hence, an all-$B$ labor force, with cost w_BL, is cheaper than the mixture. An all-W labor force has a cost $w_W(1)L$ and then $w_W(1)L \geqq w_BL$, so the all-W labor force is at any rate no less costly; if $w_W(1) = w_B$, the two extreme cases are equally cheap.

(b) $w_W(1) < w_B$: Then if $W < L$, $w_W(W/L)W + w_BB \geqq w_W(1)W + w_BB > w_W(1)(W+B) = w_W(1)$ L; the all-W labor force is cheaper than any other labor force.

Hence, if $w_W(1) > w_B$, every firm will find it cheapest to select an all-B labor force, and if $w_W(1) < w_B$, every firm will minimize cost by hiring an all-W labor force. But equilibrium requires full employment of both types of workers. The equilibrium then requires $w_W(1) = w_B$. But even then no firm will hire both W and B workers. At equilibrium every firm is segregated, but then the only observed wage for W workers is for those in all-W firms, i.e. $w_W(1)$, which is equal to w_B. Therefore, discrimination by W workers will not result in market wage differentials but instead does result in segregation.

In technical terms, the function, $C(W, B)$ is not a convex function, specifically, the isocost curves in W-B space are not concave to the origin. Convexity implies a tendency to the middle, to compromise; but here we have a rushing to extremes. We also have the characteristic implication of nonconvexity, a dispersion of firms with basically identical market opportunities into discrete niches.

Now, in going back over the analyses of Section 2, it can be observed that the case just discussed, of discriminatory tastes by a perfect substitute group of workers, is strikingly similar to that of discriminatory tastes by workers of a complementary type, the "foremen" of our example. Though a detailed analysis of the nonconvexities in this case has not yet been made, it is clear that the profit function defined by (9) is not in general a concave function. Rather, the surface

18

defined by profits as a function of W and B has holes scattered through it. Hence, it is at least possible that for certain values of w_W and w_B and some equilibrium relation, $w_F(W/L)$, there are several distinct points of maximum profits. Equilibrium on the three labor markets (W, B, and F) may be achieved by different amounts of these, even though each firm has the same production function and each faces the same wages for W and B and the same relation between w_F and W/L. Thus, there will be a partial segregation by firms.

The relation (10) stated earlier still holds for each firm, so the previous conclusions remain valid.

We can now reconsider the theory of employer discrimination. The utility function, $U(\pi, B, W)$, depends, it has been assumed, only on the ratio B/W. But it is shown in the Appendix that such a utility function cannot possibly have convex indifference surfaces everywhere.[9] Therefore it is possible and in fact likely that in the short run equilibrium will require the coexistence of firms of different sizes with different W/B ratios, even if all firms have the same utility function. Thus at least partial segregation is a likely outcome of the utility-maximization theory. All the firms will have to have the same utility, so that the larger firms will be those with the larger proportions of W workers since utility increases with π and with W/B.

In the long run, indeed, it can be seen that with constant returns to scale, there must be perfect segregation and equality of wages. For suppose there is not perfect segregation, i.e. there is at least one firm hiring both B and W workers. For that firm, $d_B > 0$ and $d_W < 0$. Since MP_L is constant in the long run, it follows from the preceding section that all B workers will be in firms with the smallest d_B and all W workers in firms with the (algebraically)

[9] The nonconvexity that arises when only ratios matter is of importance in the theory of pollution also. For the characteristic situation there is that the pollutee is faced with consuming air or water in which the proportion of pollutants is given to him.

19

smallest d_W. Then all firms have the same d_B and same d_W and therefore all have the same W/B ratio. The equilibrium values of w_W and w_B will be $MP_L - d_W$ and $MP_L - d_B$ respectively, where MP_L is the long-run marginal product of labor, a constant. But then any firm which increases its B/W ratio slightly can make positive profits; by increasing its scale, it can make indefinitely large profits with only a slightly altered W/B ratio. It would therefore have a higher utility, so we have a contradiction to the existence of equilibrium with at least one integrated firm. Hence, all firms are segregated. In an all-B firm, $d_B = 0$, for an increase in B does not change the W/B ratio and therefore leaves utility unchanged. Similarly, in an all-W firm, $d_W = 0$. It follows that, as in the case of discrimination by substitutes, the long-run equilibrium is one of perfect segregation and equal wages.

The corresponding analysis for discrimination by complementary employees has not been worked out. It can be conjectured, though, that segregation plus possibly competition among foremen with varying discriminatory tastes will greatly weaken wage differentials.

3. COSTS OF ADJUSTMENT

Utility-maximization theories, then, provide a coherent and by no means unreasonable account of the effect of discriminatory tastes on the market in the short run. Yet they become unsatisfactory in the long run. I propose as a possible explanation that long-run adjustment processes do not work as perfectly as they are usually assumed to. When there are significant nonconvexities, the adjustment processes called for must be very rapid indeed; marginal adjustments are punished, not rewarded. In the case of discrimination by substitute workers, the firm would have to be willing to fire its entire all-W labor force and replace it by an all-B labor force or vice versa in response to a very small change in wages. It is not unreasonable to assume that there are costs, not ordinarily taken account of, which will restrain the firm from being quite so free in its adjustment behavior.

Now the idea that adjustment is costly has appeared in several diverse areas of economics. The costs of growth enter explicitly in some versions of the dynamic theory of the firm.[10] That is, the growth of the firm imposes a cost which depends on the rate of growth and which is additional to the purchase of capital goods.

The same principle, that capital costs of an unconventional kind play an important role in economic behavior and decisions, has been applied to the study of labor turnover, a problem more closely connected with ours. Operations researchers, in trying to draw up plans for hiring personnel, have incorporated in their models a fixed cost of hiring an individual. Sometimes it is also held that there is a cost attached to firing as well. These costs are partly in administration, partly in training. Even workers who have already been generally trained in the kind of work to be done must learn the ways of the particular firm. This approach, it has been argued by some, has important general economic implications; it implies that firms should not adjust their labor force to cyclical shifts in demand, since they then may incur both hiring and firing costs, costs that are avoided if the worker is retained during slack periods. Workers are being held in employment even though they contribute little to output to avoid the costs of rehiring them in the expected future boom. I do not know whether this explanation is in fact adequate but merely note that it is seriously considered.

A similar consideration may well explain why the adjustments which would wipe out racial wage differentials do not occur or at least are greatly retarded. We have only to as-

---

[10] See Edith Penrose, *The Theory of the Growth of the Firm* (Oxford: Oxford University Press, 1959); and Robin Marris, *The Economic Theory of 'Managerial' Capitalism* (Cambridge: Cambridge University Press, 1964).

sume that the employer makes an investment, let us call it a *personnel investment*, every time he hires a worker. He makes this investment with the expectation of making a competitive return on it; if he himself has no discriminatory feelings, the wage rate in full equilibrium will equal the marginal product of labor less the return on the personnel investment. Let us consider the simplest of the above models, that of discrimination by fellow employees who are perfect substitutes. If the firm starts with an all-W labor force, it will not find it profitable to fire that force, in which its personnel capital has already been sunk, and hire an all-B force, in which a new investment has to be made, simply because B wages are now slightly less than W wages. Of course, if the wage difference is large enough, it does pay to make the shift.

Obviously, in a situation like this, where there are costs to change, history matters a good deal. A fully dynamic analysis appears to be very difficult, but some insight can be obtained by study of a very special case. I here present only the results; the argument will be found in an earlier paper.[11] Suppose initially there are no B workers in the labor force. Then some enter; at the same time, there is an additional entry of W workers, and some new equilibrium emerges. Under the kinds of assumptions we have been making, a change, if it occurs at all, must be an extreme change, but there are now three kinds of extremes, or corner maxima. The typical firm may remain segregated W, though possibly adding more W workers; it may switch entirely to a segregated B state; or it may find it best to keep its present W workers while adding B workers. In the last case, of course, it will have to increase the wages of the W workers to compensate for their feelings of dislike; but it may still find it profitable to do so because replacing the existing W workers by B workers means wasting a personnel investment. If we stick closely to the model with all of its artificial conditions, we note that only the all-W firms are

[11] Arrow, "Some Models of Race in the Labor Market," Section E.

absorbing the additional supply of W workers, so that there must be some of those in the new equilibrium situation. On the other hand, there must be some firms that are all-B or else some integrated firms whose new workers are B's in order to absorb the new B workers. It can be concluded in either case, however, that there will always remain a wage difference between B and W workers in this model. Further, there will be some segregated W firms. Whether the remaining firms will be segregated B or integrated depends on the degree of discriminatory feelings by W workers against mixing with B workers.

I have not worked out the corresponding analysis for the case where there are several types of workers with different degrees of discriminatory feelings against racial mixtures in the complementary types. Nevertheless, one surmises easily that similar conditions will prevail.

The generalization that may be hazarded on the basis of the discussion thus far can be stated as follows. If we start from a position where B workers enter an essentially all-W world, the discriminatory feelings by employers and by employees, both of the same and of complementary types, will lead to a difference in wages. The forces of competition and the tendency to profit-maximization operate to mitigate these differences. However, the basic fact of a personnel investment prevents these counteracting tendencies from working with full force. In the end, we remain with wage differences coupled with tendencies to segregation.[12]

4. IMPERFECT INFORMATION

There is an alternative interpretation of employer discrimination. It can be thought of as reflecting not tastes but perception of reality. That is, if employers have the preconceived idea that B workers have lower productivity than W workers, they may be expected to be willing to hire them

[12] The preceding five paragraphs have been quoted, with minor alterations, from Arrow, "Models of Job Discrimination," pp. 94-96.

only at lower wages. (Phelps has independently introduced a similar thesis.)[13] One must examine in detail the conditions under which this argument can be maintained, that is, the conditions under which the effects of these preconceptions are the same as those of discrimination in the strict sense of tastes.

First, the employer must be able to distinguish W workers from B workers. More precisely, the cost of making the distinction should be reasonably low. An employer might derive from his reading the opinion that an employee with an unresolved Oedipus complex will be disloyal to him as a father-substitute; but if the only way of determining the existence of an unresolved Oedipus complex is a psychoanalysis of several years at the usual rates, he may well decide that it is not worthwhile for him to use this as a basis for hiring. Skin color and sex are cheap sources of information. Therefore prejudices (in the literal sense of pre-judgments, judgments made in advance of the evidence) about such differentia can be easily implemented. School diplomas undoubtedly play an excessive role in employer decisions for much the same reason.

Second, the employer must incur some cost before he can determine the employee's true productivity. If the productivity could be determined costlessly, there would be no reason to use surrogate information, necessarily less valid even under the most favorable conditions. I suppose, therefore, that the employer must hire the employee first and then incur a personnel investment cost, as discussed in the last section, before he can determine the worker's productivity. This personnel investment might, for example, include a period of training, only after which is it possible to ascertain the worker's productivity; or indeed it may be only a period of observation long enough for reliable determination of productivity. In the absence of a personnel investment cost, after all, the employer could simply hire

[13] See Edwin S. Phelps, "The Statistical Theory of Racism and Sexism," *American Economic Review*, 62 (1972), 659-661.

everyone who applied and fire those unqualified, or pay them according to productivity.

Third, it must be assumed that the employer has some idea or at any rate preconception of the distribution of productivity within each of the two categories of workers.

The simplest model to bring out the implication of these assumptions seems to be the following. Suppose there are two kinds of jobs, complementary to each other, say unskilled and skilled. All workers are qualified to perform unskilled jobs, and this is known to all employers. Only some workers, however, are *qualified* to hold skilled jobs. The employers need make no personnel investment in hiring unskilled workers but must make such an investment for skilled workers. The employer cannot know whether any given worker is qualified; however, he does believe that the probability that a random W worker is qualified is p_W and that a random B worker is qualified is p_B. An employer will eventually know whether or not a worker hired for a skilled position is in fact qualified, but this information is not available to other employers. He thus can count on keeping the qualified workers he hires.

Let r be the necessary return per worker on the personnel investment for skilled jobs. If a W worker is hired, then with probability p_W he is qualified; his productivity is MP_S, the marginal productivity of skilled workers, but the employer must pay a wage, w_W, so that the net gain to the employer is $MP_S - w_W$. On the other hand, if the worker hired turns out to be unqualified, the employer receives nothing. Hence, the expected return to a W worker hired is $(MP_S - w_W)\, p_W$. If the employer is risk-neutral, this must be equal to r. Similarly,

$$(13) \qquad r = (MP_S - w_B)\, p_B,$$

and therefore,

$$(14) \qquad w_W = q\, w_B + (1 - q)\, MP_S,$$

where $q = p_B/p_W$. Thus, if, for any reason, $p_B < p_W$, w_W is a weighted average of w_B and MP_S and therefore lies between them; since from (13) we must have $w_B < MP_S$ (in order that the employer recoup his personnel investment), it follows that $w_W > w_B$, i.e. the effect of the differential judgment as to the probability of being qualified is reflected in a wage differential.

If there are price rigidities which prevent w_B from falling much below w_W, the same forces may be reflected in a refusal to hire B workers at all for skilled jobs.

Once we shift the explanation of discriminatory behavior from unanalyzable (or at any rate unanalyzed) tastes to beliefs, we are led to seek to explain these beliefs. One possible explanation runs in terms of theories of psychological equilibrium, of which Festinger's theory of cognitive dissonance is one of the most developed.[14] The argument is that beliefs and actions should come into some sort of equilibrium; in particular, if individuals act in a discriminatory manner, they will tend to acquire or develop beliefs which justify such actions. Hence, discriminatory behavior and beliefs in differential abilities will tend to come into equilibrium. Indeed, the very fact that there are strong ethical beliefs which are in conflict with discriminatory behavior will, according to this theory, make the employer even more willing to accept subjective probabilities which will supply an appropriate justification for his conduct.

Finally, one can also seek explanations in which p_W and p_B differ in reality, even though the intrinsic abilities of W and B workers are identical. Such an explanation requires some further assumptions. Specifically, whether or not a worker is qualified is now taken to be the result of a decision by him, rather than some type of intrinsic ability. More specifically, a worker becomes qualified by making some type of investment in himself. In accordance with the previous assumptions, this investment must not be observable

[14] For a more theoretical analysis see Leon Festinger, *A Theory of Cognitive Dissonance* (Evanston, Ill.: Row, Peterson, 1957).

by the employer. Hence, the investments are not the usual types of education or experience, which are observable, but more subtle types of personal deprivation and deferment of gratification which lead to the habits of action and thought that favor good performance in skilled jobs, steadiness, punctuality, responsiveness, and initiative.

Finally, it must be assumed, as is reasonable, that the human capital needed to qualify cannot be acquired on a perfect capital market. It follows that the proportion of either group (W or B) who qualify is an increasing function of the gain from qualifying. In accordance with our basic assumption that there is no intrinsic productivity difference between W and B workers, we assume that the supply schedules for the two groups are the same. Specifically, let $v_W = w_W - w_U$ be the gain to a W worker from qualifying, where w_U is the wage rate for unskilled labor, and similarly let $v_B = w_B - w_U$. Then we postulate an increasing function, $S(v)$, such that,

$$(15) \qquad p_W = S(v_W), p_B = S(v_B).$$

Let MP_U be the marginal productivity of unskilled labor, so that,

$$(16) \qquad MP_U = w_U.$$

Note that MP_S and MP_U are determined by the supplies of skilled and unskilled labor and these in turn are determined by the proportions p_W and p_B. Hence, the system consisting of the equations (13), (15), and (16) plus the equation obtained from (13) by replacing B with W constitute a system of equations in the unknowns w_W, w_B, w_U, p_W and p_U.

From the symmetric formulation of the system, it is clear that there can easily be a symmetric, nondiscriminatory equilibrium, i.e. one in which $p_W = p_B$ and $w_W = w_B$. Two questions can be raised: (1) can there be other, discriminatory, equilibria? (2) is the symmetric equilibrium stable? It can be shown that (1) in fact discriminatory equilibria

27

are bound to exist, and (2) the stability of the symmetric equilibrium depends on the parameters of the problem.

(1) The multiplicity of equilibria can be seen most easily if we assume that the black labor force is small compared with the white, so that any variations in black response have only small effects on the marginal productivities of skilled and unskilled labor and therefore only small effects on the wages of white skilled and of unskilled labor and therefore on the proportion of whites who are qualified.

From (15), (13), (14), and the definition of v_B, the basic equilibrium relation for the black labor force is,

$$(17) \qquad p_B = S(MP_S - MP_U - (r/p_B)) = S_B(p_B).$$

This equation is to be solved for p_B; we shall argue it is reasonable that there will in general be more than one solution with $p_B = 0$, as well as an equilibrium at $p_B = 0$. Since we are assuming that the effect of the black choice of p_B on MP_S and MP_U is negligible, the right-hand side of (17) depends on p_B alone. The two sides of (17) are graphed in Figure 2 below. The proportion qualifying can, of course, never exceed 1, and we may suppose that no wage difference within the range considered brings it up to 1; hence S_B, the proportion of blacks qualifying, is less than p_B for p_B close to 1. On the other hand, as p_B tends to zero, the wage differential between the skill levels,

$$v_B = MP_S - MP_U - (r/p_B),$$

tends to $-\infty$. There will surely be some wage differential which will cause a zero supply of qualified labor; even if skilled jobs are very attractive, so that there will be some supply even with a negative differential, the supply will surely disappear if the wage differential becomes a sufficiently large negative quantity, for example, if wages for skilled labor become close to zero. Hence, the S-curve in Figure 2 has roughly the shape indicated. Equation (17) is satisfied when the S-curve intersects the 45° line; hence, from the diagram it is clear that if there are any intersec-

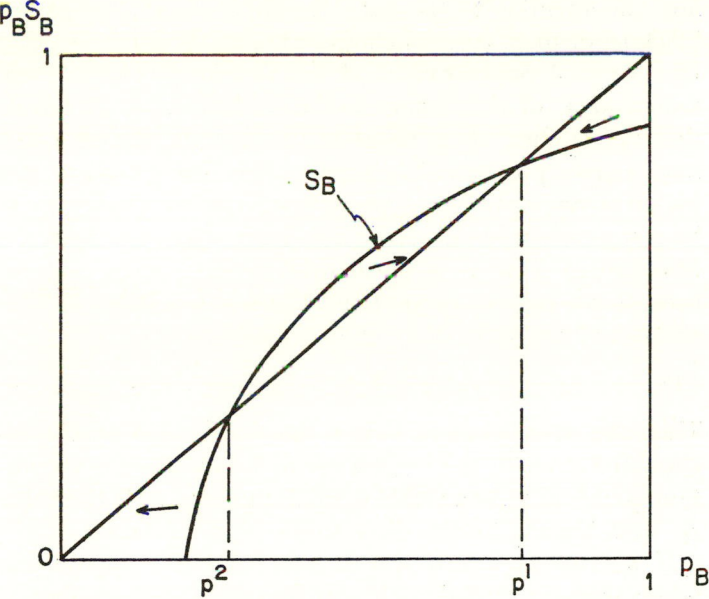

FIGURE 2

tions at all, there is more than one, so that multiple equilibria may be expected.

What happens when $p_B = 0$? Since $S_B = 0$ for p_B sufficiently small, as just argued, then $S_B = 0$ when $p_B = 0$. Hence, there must be at least three possible equilibria.

Notice that Figure 2 could also be interpreted as the diagram for analyzing the qualifying propensities of white labor force, since we are assuming that the supply function is the same for both. Hence, we see it is perfectly compatible with equilibrium conditions that p_W is at the highest intersection of the S-curve with the 45° line, while p_B is at a lower level or even zero. Thus, discrimination due to differing performance is possible even though the underlying assumptions are symmetrical with respect to race.

To discuss the plausibility of this situation, we must look into the stability of the alternative equilibria. First, we con-

29

fine our attention to the case already assumed, where the black labor force is small compared with the white, so that the marginal productivities of the two kinds of labor are independent of the behavior of the black labor force. To discuss stability, it is necessary to specify the dynamic model more precisely. We suppose that for given p_W and p_B, short-run equilibrium works itself out so quickly as to be instantaneously achieved. The basic dynamics then are Marshallian. That is, if the desired supply at any moment exceeds the current proportion qualified, the latter will increase and vice versa. In symbols,

$$(18) \qquad dp_B/dt = k[S(v_B) - p_B].$$

Then the movements of p_B are those indicated by the arrows in Figure 2; the highest possible equilibrium proportion qualified, p^1, is a stable equilibrium, and so is the value $p_B = 0$, but the intermediate value, p^2, is unstable.

If we venture a historical surmise, we may suppose that white workers started with a sufficiently large number of qualified individuals so that their proportion tended to p^1; but the black workers, starting from slavery with a low proportion qualified—a proportion correctly recognized by employers—drifted even lower toward zero or at least to some very low level. (It is unnecessary to caution the reader that this model is a gross simplification, intended to dramatize and make more extreme some existing tendencies, not to represent them literally.)

(2) We now argue that the nondiscriminatory equilibrium may be unstable. Here, we use the dynamic assumption (18) together with the same assumption for p_W; we no longer assume that the effects of black labor reactions on the whole labor market are negligible. Intuitively, we may consider a possible sequence of events, in which initially p_W slightly exceeds p_B for some reason. Then w_W slightly exceeds w_B and therefore, from (15), p_W tends to rise relative to p_B, therefore reinforcing the original disequilibrium. This verbal argument is certainly not conclusive nor very

30

convincing, and in fact the conclusion is valid only for some values of the parameters. We have to investigate the stability of the system defined by the pair of differential equations, (18), and the corresponding equation with p_B replaced by p_W, in the neighborhood of the nondiscriminatory equilibrium. While the algebra involved is elementary enough, there seems to be no way of making the result intuitively obvious. Hence, we simply reproduce the stability condition here, referring the reader for proof to an earlier paper.[15]

Let w_S be the common value of w_W and w_B at the nondiscriminatory equilibrium, p the common value of p_W and p_B. Then $v = w_S - w_U$ is the common value of v_W and v_B. Let E be the elasticity of $S(v)$ with respect to v, computed at the symmetric equilibrium value of v. From (13), $MP_S - w_S = r/p$ at the symmetric equilibrium; it is the excess of marginal product over wages for skilled workers. Then the condition for stability turns out to be that,

$$E(MP_S - w_S)/(w_S - w_U) < 1.$$

As might be expected, the greater the elasticity of the supply schedule for qualified labor, the more likely is the system to be unstable. Similarly, the greater the difference between marginal product and wage for skilled workers, the more likely is instability; this difference would be zero if there were no personnel investment costs for skilled workers, and then the system would certainly be stable. Finally, and less intuitively, the larger the wage gap between the two types of labor, the less likely is instability.

I believe these results are only the barest fragment of what could be found with better and more detailed systems in which there is an interaction between reality and perceptions of it. One must consider still more precisely how individual employers acquire knowledge which will modify their initial estimates of distributions as differing between

[15] Arrow, "Some Models of Race in the Labor Market," Section F.

groups and in turn the effects of these perceptions on the market and therefore on any incentives to modify those abilities.

APPENDIX

Nonconvexity of Indifference Maps Depending on Ratios

We suppose that employer discrimination is determined by a utility function, $U(\pi, B, W)$, where multiplying both B and W by the same positive constant leaves utility unchanged. We also assume that U is an increasing function of profits, π. It will be shown that the indifference map defined by U cannot have convex indifference surfaces; specifically, a convex combination of two indifferent points is not everywhere at least as good as either.

Choose any point (π_0, B_0, W_0). Then choose $\pi_1 < \pi_0$ (as close as needed) and B_1, W_1 so that

$$(1) \qquad U(\pi_1, B_1, W_1) = U(\pi_0, B_0, W_0).$$

From the assumptions made, (1) will continue to hold if B_1 and W_1 are reduced in the same proportion. Hence, B_1 and W_1 can be chosen arbitrarily small.

If the indifference map defined by U has everywhere convex indifference surfaces, then the average of the two points must be at least as good as (π_0, B_0, W_0). That is,

$$U(\pi', B', W') \geqq U(\pi_0, B_0, W_0),$$

where $\pi' = \frac{1}{2}\pi_1 + \frac{1}{2}\pi_0$, $B' = \frac{1}{2}B_1 + \frac{1}{2}B_0$, $W' = \frac{1}{2}W_1 + \frac{1}{2}W_0$. But then, since,

$$U(\pi', 2B', 2W') = U(\pi', B', W'),$$

we have,

$$U(\pi', 2B', 2W') \geqq U(\pi_0, B_0, W_0),$$

or, by definition,

$$U(\pi', B_1 + B_0, W_1 + W_0) \geqq U(\pi_0, B_0, W_0).$$

32

But B_1 and W_1 can be chosen as small as desired. Let them approach 0; by continuity,

$$U(\pi', B_0, W_0) \geqq U(\pi_0, B_0, W_0),$$

which is a contradiction to the assumption that U is increasing in π, since $\pi' < \pi_0$.

Melvin W. Reder   COMMENT

This paper is at least as good as the average Arrow performance, and perhaps even a little better. This is praise enough for any paper. Since the argument is developed with the author's customary skill, a discussant has scant cause to complain about details and must proceed directly to fundamentals. Before doing so, I should like to apologize at least to some members of this conference for focusing upon issues of economic theory rather than attending to more practical aspects of discrimination. However, if economists are to be of any use in everyday matters, the theory with which they operate must be in good working order. It is to this end that my comments are directed.

I sympathize fully with Professor Arrow's desire "to use as far as possible neoclassical tools in the analysis of discrimination." Where we may disagree—though I am not sure that we do—is how far these tools permit the analysis to go and how far, and in what directions, empirical observation requires it to travel.

Throughout the paper attention is directed to the effect of discrimination upon demand for labor and the resulting effect upon relative rates of compensation for (otherwise) homogeneous black and white labor service. However, virtually nothing is said about the response of labor supply to the resulting wage differential; this omission is not trivial.

Let us follow Arrow in assuming that the productive capacity of black and white workers is identical. In the same spirit let us go even further and assume that all white and black workers have identical supply functions; i.e. with given resource endowment and confronted with a given set of prices all workers would offer the same quantity of labor service per time period. Let us compare two positions: (1) an initial position of static equilibrium in which there is no taste for discrimination and in which all workers receive the same wage rate and furnish the same quantity of labor service, and (2) a position in which the same quantities as in (1) (both of black and white labor) are *supplied*, but where no employer will hire an hour of black labor service unless its wage is at least d cents per hour less than the wage of white labor. Following Arrow's notation, in (1) $w_B = w_W$ and in (2) $w_B + d \leqq w_W$.

(1) is assumed to be a position of static equilibrium where quantities L_B and L_W are both supplied and demanded. But in (2), ex hypothesi, the quantities L_B and L_W are supplied, but L_B will be demanded only at a wage rate $w_B - d$, or lower. (For simplicity, assume w_W continues to be the equilibrium wage rate for white labor.) Then, L_B will be an *equilibrium* quantity of black labor if and only if the supply of black labor has zero wage elasticity over the wage rate interval $(w_B - d)$ to w_B. A positive supply elasticity would place the equilibrium quantity of black labor in (2) below L_B; this reduction will be the greater, the greater the supply elasticity. Conversely, a positive supply elasticity of black labor would lead to an equilibrium wage for black labor in (2) that exceeded $w_W - d$; the wage would lie between w_W and $w_W - d$.

The point to be made is that the effect of labor market discrimination against a particular group of workers is not, in general, adequately measured (is understated) by a function of the difference between their equilibrium wage rate and the equilibrium wage rate of (otherwise) comparable workers not victimized by discrimination. This is because the potentially adverse effect of discrimination on the wage rate it likely to be masked in part by a reduction in the quantity of labor supplied.

In other words, the equilibrium wage differential among otherwise homogeneous workers generated by the operation of a given degree of "contact aversion" will vary inversely with the common wage elasticity of labor supply.[1] The extent of the income transfer among the two groups of workers (victims of discrimination and others) and employers will also vary with the wage elasticity of labor supply. Only in the case where this elasticity is zero may one ignore price-quantity interactions either in estimating the extent of the existing "taste for discrimination" or the income transfers which it causes.

The above remarks obviously are inspired by the theory of tax incidence. In effect I have assumed that effect of discrimination upon relative wage rates and labor quantities employed is very similar to that of a wage tax levied upon the employers of victimized workers. Tracing out the ramifications of the analysis (e.g. the effect of the reduction in the quantity of victim labor offered on the derived demand for nonvictim labor and the further repercussions on the nonvictim wage rate and labor quantity supplied) is a more or less routine exercise in the mechanics of general equilibrium theory.[2]

In a static model of the kind discussed by Arrow in Section 1 (i.e. a model where all prices are known to everyone and search costs for suppliers and/or customers are zero for everyone), labor time not offered for sale to employers must be reserved for household activity—leisure or production for own use. It would seem reasonable to interpret time reserved for household activity as time spent outside the labor force. Unemployment has no place in such a model, and it makes virtually no appearance in Arrow's paper or in Becker's dissertation.[3]

[1] If the relevant supply elasticities differ (as between victims of discrimination and other) this difference will also affect the equilibrium wage differential.

[2] One difference between discrimination resulting from employer taste and that stemming from wage taxation is that in the latter case it would be necessary to consider the effect of the government's expenditure of the tax proceeds. There are further differences between the two cases, but none seems pertinent to the matters at issue.

[3] In the introduction to the second edition, Becker remarks on this

To introduce unemployment is not a matter of great difficulty provided that the unemployment is assumed to be frictional. For this case we may amend the familiar general equilibrium model so as to permit workers three options in allocating their time: (1) gainful employment, (2) job-search or unemployment, and (3) nonmarket activity (time outside the labor force). Job search may coexist with labor market equilibrium provided the assumption of zero search cost is abandoned and we posit an average job-search period as a diminishing function of the ratio of the average reservation wage rate to the equilibrium rate. Both for realism and symmetry, we should also posit an average job-vacancy period reflecting employer search for workers.

Models with these characteristics have begun to appear in the literature.[4] While the details of their structure have not been fully explored, let me conjecture that it will be possible to develop well-behaved models with finite nonzero average job search and unfilled vacancy periods and with nonzero (steady state) stocks of unemployed workers and unfilled vacancies. In such models, employer discrimination against a particular group of workers would be reflected in some convex combination of longer search intervals (for victimized workers) for jobs at the nonvictim wage rate or lower wage rates for jobs with the same search interval. The effect would be in any case, to lower the yield to victims of discrimination per moment spent in job search.

If we assume as before an identity of labor supply functions among all workers, the effect of discrimination would be (assuming pecuniary income to be a normal good) to reduce the amount of hours per annum spent in the labor

---

omission. See G. S. Becker, *The Economics of Discrimination* (Chicago: University of Chicago Press, 1971), pp. 3-4.

[4] See, for example, the papers of Alchian, Holt, Mortensen, and Phelps in E. S. Phelps (ed.), *Microeconomic Foundations of Employment and Inflation Theory* (New York: W. W. Norton, 1969); see also M. W. Reder, "The Theory of Frictional Unemployment," *Economica*, N.S. 36 (Feb. 1969), pp. 1-27.

force. It cannot be stated a priori whether the annual time spent in job search would be increased. However, it seems plausible to suppose that the disincentive effect of discrimination would be both to increase unemployment (annual hours spent in job search) and to reduce labor force participation. If this conjecture is correct, it would provide a striking illustration of how a relative worsening of the opportunity set of a group of workers (through discrimination or otherwise) can generate qualitatively different labor supply behavior between the groups; i.e. it would explain different labor force behavior of whites and blacks without reference to (alleged) racial differences in tastes or attitudes, but simply as the result of an identical labor supply reaction to different labor market opportunities. The argument could easily be extended to cover the case where time spent in self-investment is distinguished from other uses of time; this could easily account for smaller amounts of self-investment by the victims of discrimination.

If the above conjectures are correct, recognition of the interrelation of frictional unemployment and discrimination should not create any difficulty for neoclassical theory. However (what is widely believed to be) the cyclically differential behavior of unemployment as between victims of discrimination and others does pose a challenge. It would appear that the *relative* labor market position of blacks and other victims of labor market discrimination varies in the same direction as the level of business activity.[5] For brevity

[5] Allegations to this effect may be found in James Tobin, "On Improving the Economic Status of the Negro," in T. Parsons and K. B. Clark (eds.), *The Negro American* (Boston: Beacon Press, 1965), pp. 451-457; and in L. C. Thurow, *Poverty and Discrimination* (Washington: The Brookings Institution, 1969). I have argued to the same effect in "Wage Structure and Structural Unemployment," *Review of Economic Studies*, 31 (Oct. 1964), pp. 309-323. Perhaps the most careful statements are by H. Gilman, "Economic Discrimination and Unemployment," *American Economic Review*, 55 (Dec. 1965), pp. 1077-1096, and "The White Non-White Unemployment Differential," in M. Perlman, *Human Resources in the Urban Economy* (Baltimore:

I shall refrain from commenting on the cyclical behavior of relative wage rates on different jobs and shall concentrate solely on cyclical variations in job opportunities (at given relative wage rates).

A simple interpretation of this behavior pattern is as follows: at equal wage rates most employers would prefer an additional white worker to an additional black of equal quality, provided that the delay in obtaining the white worker was not too much greater. In periods of great business activity, high employment of whites increases the delay required to hire an additional white, and some employers therefore resort to blacks to avoid excessive delay in filling jobs. In periods of lower business activity, these employers hire whites only.

There are many possible ways of rationalizing such employer behavior without departing from the spirit of neoclassical theory. Arrow's model of employer behavior with imperfect information suggests an explanation that I find attractive. According to this model, employers assign a lower subjective probability (for whatever reason) to the occurrence of a successful outcome from selecting a worker (in accord with a specified procedure) from a pool of black workers than from a pool of whites.[6] (For simplicity, assume both the *relative* probabilities of successful hire and relative black and white wage rates to be invariant with respect to the state of the labor market.) The expected utility to be derived by selecting from either racial pool will (a) increase with the subjective probability of a successful out-

---

Johns Hopkins University Press, 1963). While all of the above writers and swarms of journalists allege the same pattern of fluctuation in relative job opportunities for whites and blacks, it is not clear they are all referring to the same phenomena. Consequently while I adhere to the spirit of the allegation, caution in statement is required.

[6] Arrow restricts his argument to the case where workers acquire skill through on-the-job training. This is unnecessary: wherever the act of hiring entails cost (investment), considerations of risk (e.g. of quitting) arise.

come, (b) diminish with the wage rate paid, and (c) also diminish with the expected delay in making a hire. The expected delay in hiring either blacks or whites increases with the level of business activity, but the increase for white applicants (for comparable situations) is assumed to be greater. Consequently, the expected utility from hiring an additional worker from the black pool will rise relative to that from hiring from the white pool, and some employers will switch.[7]

The justification for postulating a greater increase in the expected hiring delay period for white workers is the assumption that it is only as full employment of whites is approached, and their hiring delay period is increased as a result, that employers begin to hire blacks.[8] The shift of hiring rates between races as business activity varies would not be expected under all circumstances. Thus if there were substantial white unemployment at the outset of a period of business expansion, what might ensue would be an increase in the rate of hiring of whites relative to blacks but with insufficient change in relative hiring delay periods to induce an increase in the rate of black hiring. Alternatively, very full employment of both races might create a situation in which relative hiring delay periods might not be affected by further business expansion.

I hold no brief for this particular model other than that it is one that can rationalize the way in which some of us believe labor market discrimination works. An essential element of this model is the assumption of an insufficient degree of wage flexibility among blacks to prevent relatively greater fluctuations in their relative employment as the level of general business activity varies. As stated, the relative wage rates for both races are fixed. But this is unneces-

[7] More precisely, employers will accept black applicants as well as white ones, and will cease to hold out for whites only.

[8] I.e., if a business expansion is sufficient to generate full employment of whites, white full employment will be reached while black employment is still increasing with business expansion.

sarily restrictive—it would suffice to posit that the relative black wage is sufficiently rigid to permit the relatively greater employment response to business conditions that we are describing. However, this is hardly a neoclassical explanation of the phenomena under discussion. Rather it is an auxiliary hypothesis grafted on to the corpus of economic theory to allow for behavior for which the theory cannot otherwise account.

A proper neoclassical explanation would not accept a racial differential in wage rigidity as a datum, but would *explain* the differential in terms of racially different costs and returns to wage flexibility.[9] So far as I am aware, no serious attempt has been made to develop such an explanation; whether it can be found is an open question. But until it is found, or until refinement of data or concepts eliminates the problem, the racially different variation in employment opportunities with business activity, will pose a challenge to economic theory.

One final point: like most economists, Arrow has analyzed the case of discrimination against a single group. But what if there is more than one group of victims? For example, consider the interrelation of discrimination against blacks and against women, among several racial and/or ethnic groups; or among any collection of such groups cross-classified by age. Obviously, the possibility of multiple bases of discrimination is no figment of the fevered imagination of a dissertation writer in search of a topic.

If we must analyze discrimination among several socially distinct groups, and especially if these groups are large enough for variations in relative numbers employed to influence relative wage rates, then the derived demand func-

---

[9] An example of neoclassical explanation of an (alleged) racial difference in behavior is the following: it is sometimes alleged that blacks have a lesser degree of future orientation than whites. But risk of property loss from criminal activity is almost surely greater for blacks and hence their expected rate of return from saving is lower than for whites.

41

tions for labor will reflect not only the state of productive technique and the supplies of nonhuman factors, but also the tastes of employers and workers for various social mixes in the work place, and the effect of these mixes on technical efficiency. In principle, the parameters of derived labor demand functions would still reflect employer utility maximization but they would also reflect the influence of a wide variety of attitudinal variables normally excluded from the theory of factor demand. Moreover, the importance of these variables would generate strong qualitative differences between the (derived) demand functions for human and nonhuman factors. It has always been the tradition for defenders of neoclassical economics to minimize the importance of such differences and for its opponents to emphasize them.

Now it is by no means obvious that the effects of employer discrimination among a plurality of socio-economic groups will be as destructive to neoclassical economics as the previous paragraph would suggest. It may be that the effects that could appear will, on close examination, vanish into the random disturbance. But by the same token, close analysis of differences in schooling quality and unmeasured inputs of the home environment may explain away part or all of the wage differences that presently appear due to labor market discrimination against blacks. Obviously, these are empirical issues.

In short, Arrow has beautifully demonstrated how neoclassical theory can analyze labor market discrimination, when discrimination does not interact with differences in labor quality. But if there is such interaction, or if there is a plurality of groups interactive in demand and all victimized by labor market discrimination, then economic theory will be less effective and more in need of sociological assistance than its adherents (among whom I wish to be counted) have hitherto believed.

Finis Welch   EDUCATION AND
RACIAL
DISCRIMINATION[1]

This is a tale of two kinds of progress. In the twentieth century there has been a pervasive improvement in the quality of schools attended by American Negroes relative to those attended by whites; and there has been an associated improvement for blacks in the income yield from schooling. My purpose is to argue that this association is causal, that improved quality has resulted in improved returns, and that discrimination against Negro education has occurred in the schools more than in the market.

It is well known that, on balance, the ability of schooling to boost Negro earnings has been less than for whites, at least for males. For example, the 1960 Census shows that for males 25 years old and over, a black eighth-grade graduate earned 73 percent as much as a white who had attended school for the same number of years.[2] For high school graduates, blacks earned 68 percent as much as whites, and the ratio falls to 62 percent for college graduates. Four years of schooling, either high school or college, increased white earnings by 40 percent, but increased Negro earnings by 30 percent. This kind of evidence has become familiar. The important question is why returns have been so much lower for Negroes. What have been the separate effects of inferior quality of schooling and of market discrimination, and how are they interrelated?

[1] The research reported here is supported by a grant from the U.S. Office of Equal Opportunity. I am indebted to Moo K. Bai, Iva Maclennan, Steve Rose, Hy Sanders, and M.P.H. Welch for their assistance.
[2] These figures are given in U.S. Bureau of the Census, *Decennial Census, Summary*, 1960, p. 590.

43

Earlier studies have placed much weight on market discrimination, arguing that measured differences in schooling quality cannot explain the comparatively much larger differences in returns.[3] But in each case these comparisons relied upon relatively recent measures of differences between black and white schools or of school achievement, and upon the "average" return to schooling for persons who attended school over a span of four or five decades. They ignored the very significant trends in increasing quality and returns which are the focal points of this paper.

In the next section the data for income returns to schooling are examined and the evidence of quality of schooling follows.

RETURNS TO SCHOOLING

Black-white differences in contributions of schooling to earnings are compared for two bodies of data. The first is the 1 in 1000 sample from the 1960 Census and the second is the 1967 Survey of Economic Opportunity (SEO). The Census data refer to the income year 1959, and SEO refers to income in 1966. Comparison is restricted to urban males who are not in the military and are not enrolled in school. The SEO data are potentially the richer source for black-white income comparisons because the sampling procedure insured a larger proportion of blacks. In the subsamples drawn, the Census contains 14,933 whites and 1,750 Negroes and SEO contains 6,892 whites and 3,443 Negroes. The SEO increased the proportion of nonwhites by adding, to a national random sample of about 30,000 individuals, a companion sample of about 20,000 persons from "poverty" areas.

[3] Two such studies are Randall D. Weiss, "The Effect of Education on the Earnings of Blacks and Whites," *The Review of Economics and Statistics*, 52, No. 2 (May 1970), 150-159, and Finis Welch, "Labor-Market Discrimination: An Interpretation of Income Differences in the Rural South," *Journal of Political Economy*, 65, No. 3 (June 1967), 225-240.

The point of departure for the income comparisons is the stratification of individual observations by race and an estimate of the time of entry into the labor force. This estimate was expressed as years of work experience.[4] The Census experience classes are: 1-4, 5-8, 9-12, and 13-25 years. For SEO, they are: 1-3, 4-7, 8-11, 12-15, 16-19, and 20-32 years. The asymmetry between the Census and SEO classes allows for comparisons of cohorts between 1959 (Census) and 1966 (SEO). For example, those with 1-4 years of experience in 1959 would have 8-11 years in 1966. The same is true of each of the final three experience classes for the two samples.

Only summary comparisons are reported in the text. Detailed income averages and regressions results are in the Appendix tables.

In Table 1, panel I refers to regression coefficients of income in arithmetic terms on the linear measure of years of school completed. No other independent variables are included, but stratification by race and experience class allows partial control for these effects. These coefficients are viewed as simple estimates of the dollar value of an additional year of schooling. For whites, the marginal value of schooling in 1959 is estimated at $521 for 1-4 years of experience. The value of schooling increases with experience, reaching a maximum of $672 in the interval 9-12 years, and

[4] In accordance with Hanoch and Mincer I assume the following ages of entry into the labor market:

Years of School Completed	0-7	8	9-11	12	13-15	17+
Age of First Year Out of School	14	16	18	20	23	28

Experience is simply current age less the estimated age at leaving school. See Giora Hanoch, "An Economic Analysis of Earnings and Schooling," *Journal of Human Resources*, 2, No. 3 (Summer 1967); and Jacob Mincer, "Schooling, Age, and Earning," in Gary S. Becker et al., *Three Essays on the Effects of Human Capital on the Personal Distribution of Income* (New York: National Bureau of Economic Research, 1972).

TABLE 1

Summary Regression Results for Coefficients of Income on Years of School Completed; Within Experience Classes for Census and SEO

I. Annual Earnings regressed on years of school completed; no other variables held constant.

Census Experience:	Black	White	SEO	Black	White
—	—	—	1-3	$598	$730
—	—	—	4-7	506	766
1-4	$259	$521	8-11	404	691
5-8	260	578	12-15	378	903
9-12	264	672	16-19	397	824
13-25	143	618	20-32	282	712

II. Natural log of annual earnings regressed on years of school completed; holding years of experience (within classes) constant.

Census Experience:	Black	White	SEO	Black	White
—	—	—	1-3	.52	.30
—	—	—	4-7	.26	.19
1-4	.25	.18	8-11	.19	.15
5-8	.17	.13	12-15	.12	.13
9-12	.10	.12	16-19	.14	.15
13-25	.06	.09	20-32	.10	.11

III. Natural log of annual earnings regressed on years of school completed; holding years of experience (within classes) and *weeks worked* last year constant.

Census Experience:	Black	White	SEO	Black	White
—	—	—	1-3	.24	.16
—	—	—	4-7	.13	.11
1-4	.08	.09	8-11	.07	.07
5-8	.08	.08	12-15	.06	.08
9-12	.07	.08	16-19	.06	.08
13-25	.04	.06	20-32	.04	.06

SOURCE: The reported data are least squares regression coefficients for urban males who are not in school and not in the military in the Census and SEO samples. The data are stratified by the indicated experience classes and by white and Negro.

declines to $618 for the experience class 13-25 years. The profile of the value of schooling over experience classes is similar for whites and blacks in the sense that the maximum occurs in the same experience interval, but the black profile is much flatter. In comparison to whites, the relative value of schooling declines monotonically with experience. This is the vintage effect. The marginal value of schooling is one-half as large for blacks as for whites in the 1-4 year experience interval, but declines to one-fourth for the 13-25 year interval.

The decline in the relative value of schooling for blacks as experience increases is consistent with many phenomena. The most likely explanations are:

1. The relative quality of schooling has been improving rapidly for blacks. Those of more recent vintage attended better schools, and the returns to schooling quality are reflected in income.

2. Labor market discrimination is diminishing through time. The labor market operates so that a major part of a person's career profile is determined at the time he enters the market. More recent entrants face less discrimination and therefore realize income profiles that are relatively higher in comparison to "white" or norm profiles.

3. One feature of market discrimination is that its effects accumulate over the life-cycle. Discrimination serves more as an impediment to advancement or promotion on-the-job, than as an impediment to finding a job in the first place.

The first two explanations are statistically identical insofar as income comparisons are concerned. It does not matter whether quality is in fact inferior or whether employers "discriminate" and act as though it is inferior. In either case, lower income results. This vintage view of discrimination, either on-the-job or in-school or both, is essentially an optimistic view, for it asserts a positive trend of declining discrimination.

47

The third explanation is essentially different from the first two. It says nothing of changes in the level of discrimination through time. Instead, it simply asserts that the impact of discrimination increases over the life-cycle. This is the pessimistic view.

A single cross-sectional analysis is incapable of distinguishing the vintage view, that asserts a secular decline in discrimination, from the life-cycle view, that argues for an increasing impact over the life-cycle. To make the distinction, comparison of the two or more cross-sections is relevant. Table 2 contains this comparison, drawn from panel

TABLE 2

The Relative Value of an Additional Year of Schooling at Each Experience Level in 1959 and in 1966

Years of Experience in 1959	Marginal Value of Schooling (Black/White)	Years of Experience in 1966	Marginal Value of Schooling (Black/White)
—	—	1-3	.82
—	—	4-7	.66
1-4	.50	8-11	.58
5-8	.45	12-15	.42
9-12	.39	16-19	.48
13-25	.23	20-32	.40

SOURCE: Panel I, Table 1.

I of Table 1. This comparison casts strong support for the vintage view of discrimination. By 1966, blacks with 1-3 years of experience had realized four-fifths as much additional income from schooling as did whites, whereas only seven years earlier the most recent black entrants into the labor market (1-4 years experience) derived only one-half as much extra income from schooling. In 1966, as in 1959, the relative value of black schooling declined with experience (except for the anomalous 16-19 class). But the most important

48

comparison is between those with 1-4 years of experience in 1959, and those with 8-11 years seven years later, and so on for 5-8 in 1959 and 12-15 in 1966; 9-12 (1959) and 16-19 (1966); and 13-25 (1959) and 20-32 (1966). For the first cohort, the life-cycle explanation predicts a decline over the seven years in the relative value of schooling from .50 to about .39. The vintage view would hold the 1959 ratios constant. In fact, for three of the four comparisons, the relative value of schooling actually increased between 1959 and 1966, and for the class in which relative value declined, the decline is considerably less than a life-cycle argument would predict.

The remaining parts of Table 1, panels II and III, each report regression coefficients when the natural logarithm of income is regressed upon years of schooling. In addition to the control secured by stratification according to race and experience, a linear measure of years of experience within each interval is included, and, in panel III, weeks worked is also held constant. It is well known that weeks worked or "job security" increases with schooling. Note that 1959 was a year of abnormally high unemployment, and the advantage of greater job security, being associated with schooling, is greater in periods of high unemployment than in "normal" periods. Thus, I adjust for weeks worked in panel III. Coefficients in this panel should be viewed as something of an understatement, but the coefficients of panel II should similarly be viewed as overstatements of returns.

In both panels II and III, the schooling coefficients are estimates of the proportionate increase in income associated with an additional year of schooling. These coefficients tell pretty much the same story as panel I. As a fraction of income, the contribution of schooling diminishes with experience, both for whites and blacks in 1959 and in 1966. The proportional contribution of schooling to income is greater for blacks than whites at low levels of experience, but falls below that enjoyed by whites as experience increases. No-

49

tice that at relatively low levels of experience the effect of holding weeks constant is greater for blacks than whites. Further, for both blacks and whites, the effect of holding weeks constant declines with experience, suggesting that the work stability phenomenon is more important at low levels of experience.

The important evidence of the three panels is that, even though the value of schooling in absolute terms is less for blacks than whites, as a proportion of income, the return is greater at more recent vintages. This suggests that as of 1966 the *rate of return* to schooling may have been higher for black than white youth. Also, the increase in the relative value of schooling for more recent vintages supports a view of diminishing discrimination.

The most impressive evidence of convergence is presented by Richard Freeman in a paper focusing upon college graduates.[5] He reports that in the most recent period, black college graduates have shifted substantially from the service professions into engineering and business related professions. Freeman also points out a very recent trend of largely white-dominated corporations to recruit actively on college campuses that are predominately black. For twenty-one colleges and universities where recruitment visits averaged 4 in 1960, the average was 50 in 1965, and 297 in 1970.

As I noted earlier, it is not possible to separate the effects of improving opportunities to younger blacks due to declining discrimination in the market from the results of declining discrimination in schools. In the next section, I discuss the available evidence on schools for Negroes. The purpose is to suggest that throughout the twentieth century the quality of these schools has been improving relative to those attended by whites. The cumulative effects of this drift can, in principle, be large, and I think they play a

[5] See Richard B. Freeman, "Discrimination Against College Educated Blacks," unpublished paper, Department of Economics, University of Chicago, 1971.

major role in explaining the strong vintage component in the return to schooling.

SCHOOLS FOR NEGROES[6]

The story of schooling for the American Negro is brief. Slave insurrections in the early part of the nineteenth century led to the legal proscription of formal instruction. By 1835 every southern state had a law prohibiting the schooling of slaves, and some even forbade instruction of freedmen. Emancipation thus came at a time when no slave under thirty years old could legally have been schooled. In 1860 seven-eighths of the Negro populace was enslaved. Bond estimates that at this time not more than 5 percent of the total black population was literate.[7]

A century has passed, but these events cast a shadow that outlives a single generation. Consider the average black male 25 years old or older in 1959, whose proportionate income-increment from schooling falls short of that received by the average white. In 1959, the year of the income comparison, this average man was 47 years old, having been born in 1912. If we assume a 25-year generation span, his father was born in 1887, and in 1862 his grandfather was born a slave. His great grandparents, having been born under proscription, would have been unschooled. The grandfather, were he one of the 10 percent who attended school at all, would most likely have been instructed by a missionary, in a school operated by the Freedmen's Bureau. His father would have entered school as the brunt of disfranchisement was tearing even wider gaps between the quality of black and white schools; and our average black man him-

[6] I have gained from my reading of a chapter in Richard Freeman's forthcoming book, *Black Elite* (N.Y.: McGraw-Hill, 1973), which discusses the drastic changes in relative expenditures on Negro pupils following disfranchisement.

[7] See, H. M. Bond, *The Education of the Negro in the American Social Order* (New York: Octagon Books, 1966).

self would have attended school sometime between World War I and the Great Depression, during an agrarian depression that had its full impact on the rural South.

Until emancipation, most Negroes who attended school were freedmen in the North, and they accounted for less than 2 percent of the school-age population. The effective origin of mass Negro education in the South was during and immediately following the Civil War. Following the securing of a southern city by Union forces during the war, missionary societies were encouraged to open day schools for the "contraband of war."[8] The first such school was established in 1861, only six months after the beginning of hostilities. In this manner schools were established in Virginia and in North and South Carolina. After the end of the war, the pattern continued with the Army assuming funding responsibilities via local taxes and tuition, and church groups or missionary societies recruiting staff.

This effort retained its form but was magnified during the reign of the Freedman's Bureau. The Bureau typically financed construction (of something like 4,250 schools) while staffing was left to the church. In this interval (1865-70), 9,300 teachers were employed to instruct 247,000 pupils or something like 15 percent of the total school-age population.[9] About 60 percent of revenue came from the Bureau, another 25 percent was contributed by churches, and the remaining 15 percent was tuition (usually inversely related to family earnings) and donations.[10]

[8] The term is attributed to General Butler in *ibid.*, p. 24.

[9] These data are provided in *ibid.* Notice that the attendance data are an accumulation over the five-year period; it is more likely that an average of 5-7 percent of the school-aged population was instructed in any given year.

[10] A reference to "tuition vouchers" comes from a report, "Colored Schools" by Joseph Warren to Col. John Eaton, General Superintendent of Schools for Refugees and Freedman, Memphis, Tenn., Feb. 24, 1864, U.S. Refugees, Freedmen and Abandoned Lands Bureau, *Extracts from Documents in the Office of the General Superintendent* (Memphis, Tenn.: Freedom Press, 1865).

The period of congressional reconstruction, 1867-1875, established free public education on a significant scale as can be seen from the enrollment data of Table 3.

TABLE 3

Negro School Attendance Related to School Age Population, 1850-1920

Year	No. Attending School (000)	Percent of Total Pop. 5-20 Years
1850	26	1.7
1860	33	1.8
1870	180	9.2
1880	856	32.5
1890	999	32.0
1900	1,097	31.3
1910	1,671	45.4
1920	2,050	54.0

SOURCE: H. M. Bond, *The Education of the Negro in the American Social Order* (New York: Octagon Books, 1966).

In the South, public education was not generally available for whites before the war, and appears to have been opposed by conservative or landed Democrats, who had political control. The ascension of Republicans during the post-war period brought political support for public education, financed largely through property taxes that in many cases exempted small holdings.

From the start, Negro and white children attended separate schools, but it may be that, although separate, these schools were more nearly equal than they would be at any future time. What scant data are available show that teachers' salaries and school terms were the same. It does appear, however, that pupil/teacher ratios were significantly larger in the Negro schools. Also, we have little data concerning quality of school facilities or of teachers, so the hints of relative parity *vis-à-vis* quality may be quite wrong. We only know that what little data are available contain no strong indications of quality differences.

The return to office of conservative Democrats in the elections of 1876-1877 followed the end of congressional reconstruction and waning support for public schools. There was considerable antagonism to property taxes imposed by Republican regimes, and, as tax rates were rolled back, school funds were restricted. In nine southern states, total white and Negro enrollment expanded by 33 percent between 1875 and 1880, while aggregate educational expenditures fell by 21 percent, i.e. expenditures per enrolled pupil fell 40 percent in five years.[11] This general expansion in enrollment suggests rapidly expanding demand, but it masks reactions in individual states to the return of conservative rule. Enrollment in Arkansas, for example, dropped 80 percent in a single year.[12] It seems that conservatives were opposed to publicly supported education in general, and did not especially de-emphasize Negro schools.

Throughout these early years the major distinction between white and Negro schools seems to lie in the ratio of pupils to teachers as is summarized in Table 4.

TABLE 4

Pupil/Teacher Ratios and Segregated Southern Schools—1870-1890

	1869-70	1879-80	1889-90
Negro Schools	60	58	57
White Schools	32	36	41

SOURCE: Reports of the State Superintendents of Education for Alabama, Mississippi, North Carolina, South Carolina, Texas, and Virginia.

[11] Bond, op. cit., p. 92. The states are Alabama, Arkansas, Florida, Louisiana, Mississippi, North Carolina, South Carolina, Tennessee, and Texas.
[12] Ibid., p. 90.

54

School terms, required by law to be equated in some states, were not highly differentiated and although significant black-white differences in teacher salaries were emerging by the end of the century, these differences were minor in comparison to salary differences between states.[13] While enrollment rates remained less for Negro children, the reported fractions of those enrolled in average daily attendance were very similar.[14] One characteristic of Negro and white schools in this period would persist as one of the most notable differences throughout the first third of the twentieth century. I refer to the extraordinarily high proportion of Negroes enrolled in the first grade. In Texas in 1889-1890, 20 percent of the publicly enrolled white students were enrolled in the first grade, while 37 percent of Negro pupils were enrolled in the first grade. For whites, the ratio of first to second graders was 1.41 and for Negroes 1.95. With static enrollment profiles, this ratio is an estimate of the number of years the average pupil spends in the first grade (relative to the second) and suggests retention rates for Negro pupils near 100 percent—the typical Negro student could plan to spend two years in the first grade.

Alongside a very rapid increase in the number of children attending public schools and the increasing pressure to reduce property taxes, Negro political power was being eroded as the forces of disfranchisement worked their way through the system. First, the Slaughterhouse cases decided by the Supreme Court in 1873 signaled the retreat of the federal government from questions of civil rights. The protection of the rights conferred by state citizenship was held to be the concern of the state. The Fourteenth Amendment

[13] In 1890, monthly salaries in Mississippi were $33.40 for white and $23.20 for Negro teachers. In Texas, they were $47.90 and $41.30, respectively; in North Carolina, white teachers earned $24.35 per month while Negro teachers earned $21.10.

[14] In Mississippi, for example, the proportion of blacks in average daily attendance varied from 55 to 65 percent on an annual basis, while the range for white attendance was 55 to 62 percent.

provided protection only against state action; actions of individuals were the responsibility of the state. This, of course, paved the way for a series of state actions designed to weaken the political potential of Negroes. Poll taxes played a role, and literacy tests attached to grandfather clauses were also important, but the *coup de grace* came in 1895 when Texas passed a law requiring political parties to hold primary elections. Since the Democratic party operated as a private club, there was no question of Negro participation.[15]

With the end of reconstruction, whatever equivalance had previously existed between black and white schools began eroding, and the process accelerated with disfranchisement. For example, in 1886 Mississippi passed a law that allowed state funds allocated to Negro schools to be diverted to white schools, and later the decision concerning amounts to be diverted was left to the discretion of county school boards. Since state allocations were made to the county independently of pupils' race, the effect of diverting funds to white children, on a per capita basis, was greatest whenever the ratio of black to white pupils was highest.

The results of this kind of process are highlighted in Table 5. By 1910, counties with a black majority spent from 7 to 30 times as much on white as black students, while "white" counties spent "only" 2 to 3 times as much on white pupils.

The same Mississippi law that allowed diversion of funds from Negro to white schools also provided for teacher salaries to be related to scores on examinations. From this point (1886) Negro and white teacher salaries drifted apart (see Table 6).

In Alabama, the change was belated. As late as 1890 expenditures for white pupils exceeded those for blacks by

[15] See for example, Henry A. Bullock, A *History of Negro Education in the South* (Cambridge, Mass.: Harvard University Press, 1967). Bullock offers a discussion of the several routes to disfranchisement the states used and the associated effects on the school systems.

TABLE 5

Public School Expenditures in Selected Mississippi Counties by Race, 1908-1909

County	Percent of Negro Pupils in Total Enrollment	Annual Expenditures Per Pupil Enrolled	
		White	Negro
Washington	92	$80.00	$2.50
Noxubee	86	20.00	1.69
Yazoo	73	15.00	1.83
Copiah	61	7.43	2.51
Attala	49	3.42	1.02
Greene	21	9.22	4.59
Itawamba	10	5.65	3.50

SOURCE: DuBois, W.E.B., *The Common School and the Negro American* (Atlanta: Atlanta University Press, 1910), pp. 72-77, as quoted by H. M. Bond, *The Education of the Negro in the American Social Order* (New York: Octagon Books, 1966).

TABLE 6

Average Monthly Salaries of Mississippi Teachers, Selected Years, 1875-1895

Year	White	Negro
1875	$57.50	$53.34
1885	28.74	28.74
1890	33.37	23.20
1895	33.04	21.46

SOURCE: H. M. Bond, *The Education of the Negro in the American Social Order* (New York: Octagon Books, 1966), p. 97.

only 18 percent, but in that year the provision of the state constitution of 1875 that called for *equal* school systems was modified to read *equal as nearly as practicable*. After this change, separate school statistics were not reported until

1909, by which time annual expenditures for white pupils were 6 times as large as for blacks.[16]

For practical purposes, today's black population was schooled in the twentieth century. The beginning of the century was concurrent with disfranchisement, and quality discrepancies between black and white schools were probably larger then than at any other time. Whatever evidence one selects, the implication is that the trend in this century has been toward equality.

The change that may have been of greatest importance in terms of learning acquired during the school year is the convergence in the length of school terms between urban and rural areas and between the South and other parts of the country. The evidence is that school terms have not seriously differed between whites and blacks in the segregated South. Rural areas had shorter terms than urban areas, and the South generally had shorter terms than elsewhere. But the greater concentration of blacks in the rural South implies that their school terms were shorter. Further, within the South, attendance rates are reported as being similar between whites and blacks, but were lower in the early part of the century than in the rest of the country. The combined effects of shorter terms in the rural South and of lower attendance rates gives the very large discrepancies in days attended that are reported in panel A of Table 7. Days attended per year increased from 57 to 151, a multiple of 2.6, for Negro pupils in this period, and, by the desegregation decision of 1954, there was no real black-white difference in days attended.

It is hard to imagine the impact of differences in the pupil/teacher ratio, but it is clear that they were large: in 1920, Negro teachers had one and three-quarters as many pupils as the "average" teacher in the country; by 1954 the difference had been substantially reduced. That very high pupil/teacher ratios may signal inferior quality can be seen

[16] Bond, *op. cit.*, pp. 112-113.

by examining the underlying data. In Florida in 1900 there were 1.02 teachers per Negro school with an average of 64 pupils enrolled per teacher, by 1920 there were 1.72 teachers per school and 55 pupils per teacher. In Georgia, there were 1.13 teachers per Negro school in 1900 with 57 pupils per teacher and in 1920 there were 1.41 teachers per school with a pupil/teacher ratio of 56. These examples are typical. The one-teacher school was the most common form of instruction and that teacher might be responsible for 50 to 60 children who might be enrolled in six or eight different grade-instructional levels. Clearly discipline would have consumed a significant proportion of instructional time and energy.

In examining the data of the Negro schools, the most striking dimension is the extraordinarily high ratio of first to second graders. If all students complete at least the second grade, and if there is no growth in total enrollment (southern Negro school enrollment has grown at annual rates of less than one percent each decade this century) then the ratio of enrollment of first to second graders is the time required to complete the first grade relative to the time required to complete the second. Since the second grade cannot be completed in less than one year, we can assume that on average a Negro student took at least two years to complete the first grade between 1920 and 1940.

Retention rates that average 100 percent would hardly indicate high quality education; they rather suggest low quality coupled with inflexible standards. But note in panel B of Table 7 that between 1940 and 1954 the implicit retention rates in southern Negro schools converged toward the national norm.

The same pattern of convergence, in terms of these crude measures of nominal quality, is shown in panel C of this table, both in terms of teacher salaries and total expenditures. But for expenditures the picture is even less clear than for the attendance and retention data. For quality to be proportionate to expenditures it is necessary that a dol-

59

TABLE 7

Comparisons of Twentieth Century Trends in Characteristics Between the Segregated Negro Schools, Southern White Schools, and All U.S. Schools

A. Days attended and enrollment per teacher. A comparison of segregated Negro schools to other schools 1900-1954.

Year	Average Days Attended per Pupil Enrolled		Pupils Enrolled per Classroom Teacher	
	Negro Schools	All Schools	Negro Schools	All Schools
1899-1900	57	69[a]	56.7	42.5[a]
1908-1909	71	88[a]	56.4	39.9[a]
1919-1920	80	121	56.0	31.8
1929-1930	97	143	43.7	30.0
1939-1940	126	152	45.3	29.0
1949-1950	148	158	33.6	27.5
1953-1954	151	159	32.9	27.9

B. Enrollment of public school students in first grade and implicit retention rates for first grade 1900-1954.

Year	Percent Enrolled in First Grade		Ratio of Enrollment in First to Second Grade	
	Negro Schools	All Schools	Negro Schools	All Schools
1899-1900	31.9	20.6	1.37	1.14[a]
1908-1909	28.7	19.2	1.45	1.49[a]
1919-1920	36.8	22.9	1.96	1.64
1929-1930	34.4	16.2	2.35	1.48
1939-1940	26.0	11.9	2.03	1.29
1949-1950	19.5	12.6	1.62	1.20
1953-1954	16.5	12.7	1.45	1.25

C. Teacher salaries and expenditures per pupil in average daily attendance.

Years	Salaries			Annual Expenditures per Pupil		
	Negro Schools	Southern White Schools	All Schools	Negro Schools	Southern White Schools	All Schools
1899-1900	$25/mo.	$37/mo.	—	$3	$12	$—
1908-1909	26/mo.	49/mo.	—	9	25	—
1919-1920	36/mo.	73/mo.	$871/yr.	10	43	—
1929-1930	—	—	1,420/yr.	15[b]	49[b]	87
1939-1940	601/yr.	1,046/yr.	1,441/yr.	19	59	88
1949-1950	2,143/yr.	—	3,010/yr.	—	—	209
1953-1954	2,861/yr.	3,384/yr.	3,825/yr.	110[c]	181[c]	265

D. Teacher salaries and expenditures: ratios of Negro schools to southern white schools (computed from panel C).

Years	Salaries	Annual Expenditures per Pupil
1899-1900	.68	.25
1908-1909	.53	.36
1919-1920	.52	.23
1929-1930	—	.31[b]
1939-1940	.57	.32
1949-1950	—	—
1953-1954	.85	.61[c]

SOURCES: U.S. Office of Education, *Biennial Survey of Education in the United States,* "Statistics of State School Systems," various issues. (Earlier editions are by the Bureau of Education in the Department of the Interior.) State Superintendents of Education, *Annual Reports,* various states, various years, and David Blose, "Statistics of the Education of Negroes," U.S. Office of Education, Circular No. 215, June 1943.

[a] Southern white schools only.

[b] Refers to 1931-1932 instead of 1929-1930.

[c] Instructional expenses only.

61

lar spent on a Negro school be neither more nor less effective than a dollar spent on a white school. Even if it were obvious what "effective" means in this context, it is not clear that dollars spent on the two alternatives have equal effect.

Suppose for example that Negro teachers are equal in capability to white teachers. The lower expenditure on Negro schools might reflect discrimination against Negro teachers, but would not indicate inferior quality schools. Similarly, we have no evidence that, within fairly narrow ranges, the pupil/teacher ratio affects what a pupil learns. But, if this ratio is unimportant, then variations in expenditures that refer to variations in pupils per teacher would not indicate variations in quality of schooling.

In any case the evidence of Table 7 is that, over the course of the first half of this century, segregated Negro schools were becoming increasingly similar to those attended by other American children. This presumably indicates convergence in quality of schooling.

By the time of the Supreme Court decision of 1954, ruling that segregated schools were intrinsically inferior, Negro schools were more like white schools than at any time since disfranchisement, but large and important differences remained as is clear from Table 7. Although the attributes reported there show significant differences, the greater black-white differences were in expenditures for support services. For example in 1945-1946 Mississippi discriminated more than any other southern state, spending 3.6 times as much for instruction of white as for Negro pupils. In that same year, Mississippi spent 27.5 as much per white pupil for transportation to and from school as for Negro pupils. North Carolina, apparently the least discriminatory in terms of instructional expenses, spent only 5 percent more on whites, but spent 2.4 times as much on transportation, and the ratio rises to 3.2 when all services (health, lunch programs, transportation) are combined.

But for these services, as for other attributes of the schools, the trend prior to the desegregation decision was toward equality as is demonstrated in Table 8, which shows proportions of pupils transported at public expense.

Thus in terms of nominal characteristics—pupil/teacher ratios, days attended per year, expenditures, etc.—there is remarkably consistent evidence that black and white south- ern schools were becoming increasingly similar and that this trend originated before the Second World War. Why the trend existed is beyond the scope of this paper.[17] But the question of what has happened since 1954 is, of course, very much to the point.

TABLE 8

Percentages of Southern Pupils Transported to Public Schools, 1940-1952

	1939-1940	1949-1950	1951-1952
Negro	6.3	23.6	31.6
White	37.3	44.7	45.5

SOURCE: Truman M. Pierce, et al., *White and Negro Schools in the South: An Analysis of Biracial Education* (Englewood Cliffs, N.J.: Prentice-Hall, 1955), p. 232.

Empirically, the problem becomes more difficult because the desegregation decision, with the potential for enforce- ment, served as a major impediment to *publishing* data about separate schools for Negroes. In fact, the federal gov- ernment stopped publishing these data long before the southern states. Table 9 offers sample data for Mississippi and Alabama. At the time of the desegregation decision,

[17] My own impression is that the pressure for equality came almost exclusively from the courts. As early as 1921, Missouri established out- of-state tuition programs to ward off claims that "equal" professional schools were not available, and in 1935 the NAACP led a bid for desegregation of the University of Maryland, as cited by Bullock, *op. cit.* Before 1940, segregation of most of the state-supported Southern universities had given way, and in 1942 the Supreme Court ruled that Negro and white teachers in Nashville had to be paid on a common scale.

TABLE 9

Annual Expenditures Per Pupil in Average Daily Attendance, Mississippi and Alabama, 1954-1961

	1953-1954		1957-1958		1960-1961	
	Negro Schools	*White Schools*	*Negro Schools*	*White Schools*	*Negro Schools*	*White Schools*
Mississippi	$ 43.44	$103.30	$ 86.77	$133.16	$117.10	$173.43
Alabama	142.45	162.88	190.08	216.08	201.32	231.96

SOURCE: Reports of State Commissioners of Education. State Superintendents of Education, *Annual Reports*, various states, various years.

Mississippi was spending only 42 percent as much on Negro as on white pupils, and eight years later the ratio had increased to 67 percent. Alabama had previously equated teacher salaries and pupil/teacher ratios, and, after the decision, a constant expenditure ratio (87 percent) was maintained. In Mississippi, the enrollment ratio of Negro first to second graders was 2.3 in 1954 and had fallen to 1.2 by 1961. So it does seem that the trend toward similarity was maintained. In 1961 Mississippi stopped publishing separate statistics for Negro schools, as did Alabama in 1964.

Of course, by the 1960's the terms "southern segregated schools" and "schools attended by Negroes" were no longer synonymous. In 1960 only 54 percent of all Negro pupils attended southern schools. Until the *Coleman Report*, we had almost no data for schools attended by Negroes outside the South.[18] What data there are suggest that these schools have been "better" than the southern schools the migrants left. The Coleman data are clear on this score, especially when considering measures of teacher performance.

A summary of the shifting geographic distribution of America's Negro population is provided in Table 10. In

[18] James S. Coleman et al., *Equality of Educational Opportunity* (Washington, D.C.: U.S. Government Printing Office, 1966).

TABLE 10

Region of Residence of the U.S. Negro Population 1900-1960

Percent Living In —	1900	1930	1960
South:			
Urban	13.9	24.9	32.7
Rural	76.1	53.8	23.5
North & West	10.0	21.3	43.8

SOURCES: Data for 1960, Census from U.S. Bureau of the Census, *Decennial Census*, various issues. Earlier data, Negro Year Book as cited by H. M. Bond, *The Education of the Negro in the American Social Order* (New York: Octagon Books, 1966).

sixty years the proportion of Negroes living in the South fell from 90 to 56 percent. Increasingly, the American Negro either left the South or, if he stayed, moved to urban areas. Either move raised the quality of the schools his children attended.

Let us turn now to the evidence of quality of teachers and of pupil achievement.

Teachers

The data on school completion levels for southern Negro teachers are surprisingly good and are summarized in Table 11. In 1930, 38 percent of the Negro teaching force had not graduated from high school, and another 20 percent had completed less than two years of college. The rate of increase in average schooling of teachers is perhaps greatest among the several attributes we have examined. In 1930, 9 percent of Negro teachers had the equivalent of a bachelor's degree; by 1952 the proportion had risen to 73 percent. This compares favorably with the 78 percent of southern white teachers who were college graduates at that time.

It is likely that increased schooling of Negro teachers improved the quality of the instructional services provided to

TABLE 11

School Completion Levels of Public School Teachers in Segregated Southern Schools 1930-1952

	1930	1939-1940		1949-1950		1951-1952	
Percentage of Teachers Who Had Completed	Negro Schools	Negro Schools	White Schools	Negro Schools	White Schools	Negro Schools	White Schools
a) Less than two years of college	58	30	7	14	6	9	3
b) Four or more years of college	9	35	60	65	72	73	78

SOURCE: Fred McCuistion "The South's Negro Teaching Force," *Journal of Negro Education*, 1, No. 1 (April 1932), 20; and Truman M. Pierce et al., *White and Negro Schools in the South: An Analysis of Biracial Education* (Englewood Cliffs, New Jersey: Prentice-Hall, 1955), p. 201.

Negro pupils. We have evidence that measured teacher verbal capacity is directly related to increments in pupil achievement, and we also have data suggesting that the measured school achievement of teachers rises with the amount of time they have spent in school attendance.[19]

In 1930 Bond, in a comparison to the Rosenwald Survey of Achievement of Southern Negro Pupils, administered the Stanford Achievement test (the same instrument used for children) to 306 teachers in six counties of Alabama.[20] He found that median performance of teachers who had not graduated from high school was equivalent to 7.6 years of

[19] For further evidence that measured teacher verbal capacity is directly related to increments in pupil achievement, see Erick Hanushek, "Teacher Characteristics and Gains in Student Achievement: Estimation Using Micro-Data" *American Economic Review*, 61 (May 1971), 280-298.

[20] Bond, *op. cit.*

school achievement; for those who had graduated from high school, but had less than two years of college, achievement was equivalent to 8.0 school years; and, for those with two or more years of college, median achievement was 9.1 years. The very low levels of these scores reflect in part the earlier period when the teachers would themselves have been schooled. Bond, on an optimistic note, pointed out that "an arrangement of scores by the ages of the teachers tested indicated that scores in achievement advanced as age of teacher declined, leading one to believe that the younger generation of Negro teachers is more able than the older generation."[21]

Although there are more recent comparisons of teacher performance on exams, the normalization procedures do not allow direct comparison with the Bond survey. Coleman provided convincing evidence that teachers of Negro pupils (which by 1965 did not refer exclusively to Negro teachers) are not as verbally adept as those of white pupils.[22] His data, from a 30-question reading test, are summarized in Table 12. A little over one-half of all Negro pupils attended school in the South, where teacher scores are lowest. The test score discrepancies are obviously significant and point to the disadvantage Negro pupils faced in 1965. Unfortunately, I cannot translate these scores into terms that would allow comparison to the scores for 1930 because the translation from percentage accuracy on tests to years completed equivalence is non-linear. For example, the Coleman data for children show that the median score for Negro sixth graders in metropolitan areas of the South is 85 percent of the national average, but they are 1.9 years below the norm. Therefore, expressed in terms of standard school years, these pupils achieve only 69 percent of the norm.[23]

[21] *Ibid.*, p. 277.

[22] See Coleman, *op. cit.* In 1965, 65 percent of Negro elementary and 59 percent of Negro high school students had Negro teachers, whereas 2 percent of white pupils had Negro teachers.

[23] Greene, using tests administered in 1960, reports that Negro

67

TABLE 12

Scores on Verbal Facility Tests Given to Teachers of Negro Pupils as a Percentage of the National Average Score Received by Teachers of White Children, Fall 1965

Region	Elementary	Secondary
South		
Metropolitan	82	88
Non-Metropolitan	75	83
North and West	91	94
All Regions	87	91

SOURCE: James S. Coleman et al., *Equality of Educational Opportunity* (Washington, D.C.: U.S. Government Printing Office, 1966).

Bond's data show that achievement levels of Negro teachers were low in 1930. He also noted that achievement is positively related to schooling, and he asserted an inverse relation between achievement and teacher vintage, more recently trained teachers appearing more "able." On each count there is reason for optimism. But Coleman found that in 1965—after differences in school completion levels had vanished—large discrepancies remained between verbal abilities of teachers of Negro and white pupils. Equality may be just around the corner, but it seems to be a fairly long block.

---

teachers in "a large southeastern city" score 82 percent as many points as white teachers. This is the same ratio that Coleman reports for teachers of Negro pupils in metropolitan areas of the South. The score distribution of white teachers dominated the Negro distribution: only 6 percent of Negro teachers fell above the white mean while 89 percent of white teachers scored above the Negro mean. In this sample, Negro teachers had an average of 0.45 more years of schooling than white teachers, 1.5 years more experience, and earned $258 more each year. See James E. Greene, "A Comparison of Certain Characteristics of White and Negro Teachers in a Large Southeastern School System," *Journal of Social Psychology*, 58, No. 2 (December 1962), 383-391.

Student Achievement

To this point I have described nominal attributes of schools and have not focused upon the more important and vastly more difficult question of what is learned. The fact is that we do not know what it is about school attendance that increases earning capacity in later life. Evidently, existing measures of cognitive skill do not tell the whole story. It is true that measured capacity increases with years of schooling and that there is a very "significant" statistical relationship between measures of achievement and earnings. But the current evidence is that these measures of achievement account for something less than 20 percent of the estimated value of schooling.[24] Thus the existing measures of achievement give only a partial picture of the product of schooling. Whatever the weaknesses of these measures, however, there are certainly no superior alternatives now available.

With regard to achievement scores, a substantial body of evidence shows these measures to be systematically related to attributes of the school and home environment.[25] As early as 1923, Brigham, in examining scores on army intelligence tests, noted a positive relation with schooling.[26] He noted also that when persons with equal schooling were compared, "striking differences in intelligence" existed between northern and southern Negroes, and he attributed these differences, in part, to the superior quality of northern schools.[27]

[24] See Herbert Gintis, "Education, Technology, and Characteristics of Worker Productivity," *American Economic Review*, 61 (May 1971), 266-279; Zvi Griliches and W. Mason, "Education, Income, and Ability," *Journal of Political Economy*, 80 (June 1972), S74-S103; and Eric Hanushek, "Regional Differences in the Structure of Earnings," unpublished paper, Department of Economics, U.S. Air Force Academy, September 1971.

[25] See for example, Coleman, *op. cit.*; and Hanushek, "Teacher Characteristics."

[26] See Carl C. Brigham, *A Study of American Intelligence* (Princeton, N.J.: Princeton University Press, 1923).

[27] *Ibid.*, pp. 349-351.

69

Bond, in examining achievement test scores of Negro pupils in Alabama in 1930-1931, gave the schools operated by the Tennessee Coal & Iron Company as an example. These schools were operated in Jefferson County, which contains Birmingham, in settlements that included health services and improved housing. Third-grade pupils, who, according to Bond, had for the most part been born in the settlements, had achievement scores equivalent to the national norm. Sixth graders fell a full year behind norms, but Bond attributes this to their having spent only four to five years in the TCI schools. The striking aspect of these schools is that third graders surpassed other Negro pupils in the county by 0.6-0.7 years in reading capacity and sixth graders were 0.9-1.0 years ahead. In both the TCI and the Birmingham schools, third graders were retarded in terms of chronological age by 0.8-0.9 years and sixth graders by 1.3-1.4 years.

Since the data examined above show a fairly consistent pattern of black-white convergence in quality-related characteristics of schools, it is reasonable to expect convergence in measures of achievement. Unfortunately, there is a paucity of achievement data for comparisons of Negro students at different points in time. There is some evidence, however, that convergence has occurred.

The Rosenwald Survey[28]

Between 1929 and 1931 the Julius Rosenwald Fund conducted a survey of ten thousand Negro third- and sixth-grade pupils in sixteen "representative" counties of Alabama, Louisiana, and North Carolina. For third graders the national standard for the test used was 3.5 school years, and the average of the county medians in the sample of Negro pupils was 2.75 years. Furthermore, on an age-in-grade basis, these pupils were retarded an additional 1.4 years.

[28] A summary of the findings of this survey appears in Bond, *op. cit.*, pp. 339-344.

Based on chronological age, the average student should have been in grade 4.9 rather than 3.5 so that these borderline fourth-fifth year attenders scored 2.2 years below what would have been predicted for an "average" student. Sixth graders scored 4.9 school achievement years with a norm of 6.5, but their age indicated 1.5 additional years of retardation so that these pupils in their eighth year of attendance scored 3.1 years below the standard.

The Coleman Survey[29]

The 1964 Civil Rights Act required a national survey of educational opportunities within two years of enactment. The survey was conducted in 1965 by the National Center for Educational Statistics under the direction of James S. Coleman. Although the 700-page report examines many attributes of schools, pupils, and teachers, I did not find reference to age-in-grade retardation. In fact, an examination of year-to-year changes in enrollment patterns reveals little evidence of stacking at the first years of elementary and secondary school, as was characteristic of the period prior to World War II. I assume therefore that grade advancement rates were similar between Negro and white children by 1965. If so, achievement discrepancies in grade indicate total retardation. The Coleman data show that southern Negro sixth graders were 2.1 years below the norm and ninth graders were 3.0 years behind. Using the Coleman data, my interpolation for third graders gives a deficit of 0.9 years.

Therefore, in comparison to southern Negro third graders in 1930 who had attended school for 4.9 years with an achievement index of 2.75 years, linear interpolation of the Coleman data suggests that in 1965 a Negro pupil in the South who had attended school 4.9 years would have had an achievement index of 3.3 years.[30] In 1930, sixth graders

[29] Coleman, *op. cit.*

[30] In the Coleman data, retardation grew from 0.9 to 2.1 years be-

had attended school for an average of 8.0 years with an achievement yield of 4.9 years. The interpolation for 1965 suggests that the achievement yield in that year would have been 5.4 years for those who had eight years in attendance.

Obviously these imputations are subject to error, but they may indicate real gains per attendance year for Negro pupils. The underlying data simply show that in 1930 southern, black, third and sixth graders were somewhere between 0.1 and 0.5 year closer to national norms than in 1965. But this advantage had been purchased at the expense of one and one-half extra years of attendance.

Some added evidence of improved relative school performance for Negro pupils is offered by Hansen, who was superintendent of schools in Washington, D.C., in the period following desegregation.[31] He notes that in 1955-1966 third-grade class medians ranged from 1.1 to 1.4 years below norm and sixth grade scores were 1.3 to 1.6 years behind, this when 66 percent of the school population was Negro. By 1958-1959, when the proportion of Negro pupils had risen to 75 percent, third-grade classes had reduced the deficit so that the range of class medians was then from 0.5 to 0.6 year below the norm and sixth graders were 0.0 to 0.5 year behind. This is an example of a response achieved under a fairly intensive campaign to improve the quality of schooling, but it may not be a completely isolated example.

The Board of Education in New York City annually gives nationally standardized reading tests to third- and sixth-grade pupils, and school average scores are available. Table

---

tween the third and sixth grades, or by 0.4 per year. Projecting from grade 3.2 (Coleman exams were in the Fall) to 4.9 indicates a growth in the deficit of .68 years (0.4 × 1.7), giving a total deficit of 1.6 years in the 4.9 school year.

[31] For added evidence of improved relative school performance for Negro pupils, see Carl F. Hansen, "The Scholastic Performance of Negro and White Pupils In the Integrated Public Schools of the District of Columbia," *Harvard Educational Review*, 30, No. 3 (Summer 1960), 216-236.

13 summarizes scores for black students for selected years between 1957 and 1969. Since only class averages are available, these scores are averages for de facto segregated schools, those with the highest proportions of Negro students. Once again, the story of reading score differentials is pretty much the same as for the segregated southern schools.

TABLE 13

Black Reading Scores by Grade Level in De Facto Segregated New York City Schools, 1957-1969

Year	Grade In Which Test Was Administered	
	3rd	6th
1957	2.67	4.88
1960	2.87	5.22
1965	3.19	5.67
1969	3.31	5.38
National Average	3.5	6.5

SOURCE: The Board of Education of New York City, unpublished data. These data are weighted averages of school reading score averages within each class. Scores are normalized to allow for year-to-year variation in the time the test is administered.

The criterion for selecting schools for these computations varied from year to year as data availability permitted. The object was to select a modest number of reasonably large schools with the largest proportions of black students. The third-grade data refer to from 21 to 28 schools, each having 700 or more pupils with at least 90 percent black. The sixth grade data are for the same schools, except that in 1965 and 1969 only eleven of these elementary schools had sixth grades.

Viewed in absolute terms, scores of Negro children fall behind the norms, and these differences compound as years completed increase. Whatever forces result in differences by the third grade, these appear to continue to operate until the sixth. The important evidence lies in the trend between

73

1957 and 1969. For third graders, a 0.8 year reading deficit eroded to 0.2. In twelve years, black third graders in New York City improved an average of 0.6 year in reading achievement. This is reason for optimism. The story for the sixth grade is equally impressive: the deficit falls from 1.6 to 1.1 years.

Certainly the gain for sixth-grade blacks from 4.9 to 5.4 years is important, but the norm is 6.5, and the deficit remains large. Notice that children in the sixth grade in the spring of 1969 would have entered school no later than fall of 1963, and would therefore have missed the Headstart programs. Also, given the rapid rise in black school-completion levels, the average education levels of parents of black third graders in 1969 would have exceeded the average schooling of parents of black sixth graders so that these increments may refer in part to changes in home environment.

The fragments of evidence tell a consistent story: schools for Negroes may be inferior to those for whites and much improvement is still in order, but the record is undeniable. Improvement has occurred. To ignore this in contrasting returns to schooling between blacks and whites is misleading. In comparison to whites, the income blacks have derived from schooling is low, especially for those who attended school before 1954. For those in school after 1954, the return is more attractive, and evidence indicates this may be the product of more equal schools.

SUMMARY AND CONCLUSIONS

This is a story of progress. In the schools progress has been painfully slow and uneven. The ground lost in terms of racial equality with the encroachment process that began after southern Democrats returned to power in 1876-1877 may have taken the better part of a century to regain. The twentieth century has been smoother, and relative conditions have improved throughout for Negro pupils. Even so,

74

the available evidence is that large and important differences in pupil achievement persist. I have not examined the more recent disparate trends that appear to be accompanying the increasing racial isolation of central cities, with widening discrepancies in tax base between the black core and the white suburban ring of today's cities. But whatever inequities have been and are now being perpetrated, one fact seems clear: either on an absolute basis or relative to whites, younger generations of Negroes have received more education per year of schooling than older generations.

Alongside the evidence of schooling quality is the consistent picture offered by the income data. Ignoring earning discrepancies attributable to weeks worked annually, I find that an extra year of schooling increases earnings of a Negro male who entered the labor force between 1934 and 1946 by only 4 percent, 2 percent less than for a similar white. In comparison, for a black man who entered the market between 1959 and 1962, an extra year of schooling contributes an extra 13 percent to earnings, or 2 percent *more* than for a similar white. Thus, it is clear that either on an absolute basis or relative to whites, younger generations of Negroes receive more earnings per year of schooling than older generations.

We cannot, on the basis of this simple association between the earnings attributable to schooling and indications of quality of schooling, make probabilistic statements about the role rising quality has played in boosting earnings. Too many confounded trends suggest competing alternative hypotheses. One attractive candidate is that market discrimination has simply been diminishing. Whatever social and political forces have allowed convergence in offerings to black and white students also have allowed convergence in offerings to black and white workers.

I do not contend that quality of schooling is the only phenomenon necessary to understand the improved earning capacity of black schooling, but I do contend that it is important. On behalf of the quality hypothesis, observe that

75

the schools data show not only that black and white schools are becoming increasingly similar but that both are improving as improvement is measured by age-in-grade retardation, pupil/teacher ratios, real expenditures, or schooling of teachers. Thus, the quality hypothesis would predict not only that young blacks fare better in comparison to young whites than do older blacks in comparison to older whites, but that young blacks and whites each fare better relative to older generations of their own races. That, pure and simple, is what the data show.

APPENDIX

TABLE 14

Average Income By Schooling and Experience

		Sample: Census (1959)			
			Schooling Class		
Experience Class		0-7	8-11	12-15	16 or more
White:	1-4	$ 770	$2,450	$3,900	$ 6,720
	5-8	2,520	3,770	5,260	8,820
	9-12	2,840	4,500	6,060	10,310
	13-25	3,850	5,320	6,943	11,210
All:	1-25	3,620	4,760	6,100	9,760
Black:	1-4	520	1,070	2,320	3,145
	5-8	1,690	1,960	3,350	4,600
	9-12	2,250	3,130	3,350	7,120
	13-25	2,630	3,090	3,780	4,330
All:	1-25	2,420	2,800	3,330	4,830
		Sample: SEO (1966)			
White:	1-3	530	2,610	5,140	8,930
	4-7	1,620	4,370	6,480	10,670
	8-11	2,830	5,780	7,220	11,150
	12-15	3,770	5,780	8,340	13,000
	16-19	3,920	6,390	8,150	13,820
	20-32	4,750	6,710	8,520	13,270
All:	1-32	4,040	5,970	7,710	11,540

TABLE 14 *(continued)*

Experience Class		Schooling Class			
		0-7	8-11	12-15	16 or more
Black:	1-3	340	1,980	3,990	6,780
	4-7	1,540	3,120	4,740	7,780
	8-11	2,110	4,030	5,210	7,125
	12-15	3,180	4,130	5,160	8,360
	16-19	3,300	4,540	5,550	9,110
	20-32	3,690	4,690	5,610	8,260
All:	1-32	3,250	4,070	5,110	8,120

TABLE 15

Regression Results for the Arithmetic Value of Earnings on Years of School Completed

		Sample: Census (1959)			
Experience Class		Average Income	Average Years of Schooling	Schooling Coefficient (Std. Error)	R^2
White:	1-4	$4,150	12.81	$521 (19)	.27
	5-8	5,615	12.65	578 (22)	.24
	9-12	6,489	12.53	672 (27)	.20
	13-25	6,654	11.45	618 (17)	.14
Black:	1-4	2,066	11.19	259 (38)	.18
	5-8	2,636	10.49	260 (31)	.21
	9-12	3,251	10.07	264 (65)	.06
	13-25	3,132	8.78	143 (17)	.07

77

TABLE 15 *(continued)*

		Sample: SEO (1966)		
Experience Class		Average Income	Average Years of Schooling	Schooling Coefficient (Std. Error)	R^2
---	---	---	---	---	---
White:	1-3	$5,261	12.65	$730 (41)	.37
	4-7	6,713	12.55	766 (41)	.29
	8-11	7,495	12.40	691 (38)	.28
	12-15	8,292	12.13	903 (51)	.28
	16-19	8,569	12.02	824 (39)	.34
	20-32	8,195	11.36	712 (30)	.16
Black:	1-3	2,880	10.71	598 (41)	.39
	4-7	3,990	11.02	506 (41)	.26
	8-11	4,613	11.00	404 (39)	.20
	12-15	4,793	10.94	378 (40)	.17
	16-19	4,950	10.15	397 (36)	.24
	20-32	4,740	9.04	282 (19)	.13

Table 16

Regression Results for the Natural Logarithm of Earnings on Years of Schooling and Experience

Experience Class		Sample: Census (1959)			
		Schooling Coefficient (Std. Error)	Experience Coefficient (Std. Error)	Standard Error of the Estimate	R^2
White:	1-4	.185 (.008)	.157 (.023)	1.13	.22
	5-8	.133 (.006)	.087 (.019)	.97	.17
	9-12	.116 (.005)	.041 (.016)	.89	.16
	13-25	.093 (.003)	.010 (.003)	1.00	.08
Black:	1-4	.259 (.044)	.112 (.098)	1.57	.15
	5-8	.167 (.026)	.098 (.076)	1.33	.14
	9-12	.097 (.027)	—.057 (.082)	1.47	.05
	13-25	.056 (.015)	.029 (.013)	1.54	.02
		Sample: SEO (1966)			
White:	1-3	.303 (.021)	.274 (.081)	1.55	.28
	4-7	.189 (.014)	.095 (.038)	1.24	.19
	8-11	.147 (.014)	.069 (.038)	1.27	.11
	12-15	.131 (.015)	.068 (.043)	1.35	.09
	16-19	.154 (.012)	.042 (.040)	1.27	.16
	20-32	.110 (.209)	—.017 (.008)	1.63	.05

79

TABLE 16 *(continued)*

Experience Class		Schooling Coefficient (Std. Error)	Experience Coefficient (Std. Error)	Standard Error of the Estimate	R^2
Black:	1-3	.522	.301	2.11	.27
		(.047)	(.127)		
	4-7	.257	.101	1.69	.13
		(.033)	(.073)		
	8-11	.188	.033	1.63	.09
		(.029)	(0.71)		
	12-15	.117	.048	1.87	.03
		(.031)	(.082)		
	16-19	.140	.065	1.49	.10
		(.022)	(.070)		
	20-32	.095	—.011	1.94	.03
		(.015)	(.014)		

TABLE 17

Regression Results for the Natural Logarithm of Earnings on Years of Schooling, Experience and Weeks Worked

Experience Class		Schooling Coefficient (Std. Error)	Experience Coefficient (Std. Error)	Weeks Worked Coefficient (Std. Error)	Std. Error of Estimate	R^2
Sample: Census (1959)						
White:	1-4	.092	.046	1.42	.58	.80
		(.004)	(.012)	(.02)		
	5-8	.080	.050	1.51	.49	.79
		(.003)	(.010)	(.02)		
	9-12	.079	.033	1.48	.52	.71
		(.003)	(.010)	(.02)		
	13-25	.061	.007	1.58	.52	.75
		(.002)	(.002)	(.01)		

TABLE 17 (*continued*)

Experience Class		Schooling Coefficient (Std. Error)	Experience Coefficient (Std. Error)	Weeks Worked Coefficient (Std. Error)	Std. Error of Estimate	R^2
Black:	1-4	.081	.020	1.32	.74	.81
		(.022)	(.046)	(.05)		
	5-8	.080	.044	1.35	.72	.75
		(.015)	(.041)	(.05)		
	9-12	.067	—.031	1.44	.58	.85
		(.011)	(.032)	(.04)		
	13-25	.043	—.001	1.46	.59	.86
		(.006)	(.005)	(.02)		
Sample: SEO (1966)						
White:	1-3	.156	.208	1.26	1.09	.65
		(.016)	(.057)	(.05)		
	4-7	.106	.039	1.53	.89	.58
		(.010)	(.027)	(.05)		
	8-11	.071	.039	1.61	.86	.59
		(.010)	(.025)	(.05)		
	12-15	.085	.009	1.91	.76	.71
		(.009)	(.024)	(.05)		
	16-19	.076	—.013	1.99	.73	.73
		(.007)	(.023)	(.05)		
	20-32	.061	—.006	2.09	.78	.78
		(.004)	(.004)	(.02)		
Black:	1-3	.235	.131	1.52	1.17	.78
		(.028)	(.077)	(1.06)		
	4-7	.135	.001	1.65	.86	.78
		(.017)	(.034)	(.05)		
	8-11	.072	.036	2.01	.50	.91
		(.009)	(.022)	(.03)		
	12-15	.062	.014	2.07	.51	.93
		(.009)	(.022)	(.03)		
	16-19	.060	.044	1.85	.68	.81
		(.010)	(.032)	(.05)		
	20-32	.042	.005	2.07	.61	.90
		(.005)	(.005)	(.02)		

81

Richard Freeman   COMMENT

Labor market developments in the 1960's (and to a lesser extent earlier) are changing the traditional picture of market discrimination against black Americans. Evidence is building of substantial improvements in the relative position of black workers and particularly, of the educated black who has long suffered the greatest relative disadvantage. Finis Welch offers us calculations supporting this "new" picture of discrimination and some interesting suggestions regarding the striking drop in black-white economic differences. Using individual observations from the 1960 census and the 1966 Survey of Economic Opportunity, Welch finds a substantial gain in the return to schooling by experience class for blacks from 1959 to 1966, and relative stability or improvement in the position of specified cohorts in the 1959-1966 period. This result corroborates the findings of my *Black Elite: Education and Labor Market Discrimination* (forthcoming), based on different data and analytic techniques. The data given in *Black Elite*[1] show:

1. A great narrowing of economic differences between black and white women in the 1950-1971 period. The ratio of income goes from 0.33 to 0.82, with the remaining differential attributable entirely to education or skill differences.

2. Noticeable improvements in the relative position of black men in the late sixties, with income ratios rising by 6 points, approaching equality (given educational levels) in the Midwest and Northeast, and unemployment differences narrowing.

[1] *Black Elite: Education Labor Market Discrimination* (N.Y.: McGraw-Hill, 1973), Chapter 1. See also "The Implication of the Changing Labor Market for Minority Workers" in C. Kerr (ed.), *Higher Education and the Labor Market* (N.Y.: McGraw-Hill, 1972).

3. An extraordinary increase in the demand for black college graduates in the late sixties, with the resultant attainment of equality in college starting salaries.

4. A rate of return to black investments in college greater than that for white investments. In 1969 the black return was on the order of 20% compared to 15% for whites.

Acceptance of Welch's and my findings raises three questions for the understanding of black-white economic differences.

1. Why the decline in racial differences? The principal causal factor on which Welch focuses is the quality of black schooling, itself dependent on the extent of market discrimination against educated blacks.

The evidence in his Table 7 demonstrates a strong upward trend in the student and other resources going to the education of southern blacks. How significant schooling quality is in accounting for improved economic position is more difficult to tell from the data. For one thing, there is no strong correspondence between the timing of income improvements and appropriate lagged improvements in schooling. There was a gain for male black workers from 1939 to 1949, relatively little advance from 1949 to 1959, and further advance in the 1960's, whereas the schooling pattern is one of reasonably continuous advance. Similarly, there is no easy way to look at the differential pattern of advance for black women with changes in school quality. The evidence in Table 13, while extremely interesting, also fails to close the case, for it is highly likely that white students in New York came from an increasingly lower socioeconomic status so that dissimilar groups are being compared over time. Nonetheless, these figures are sufficiently suggestive to merit a more detailed analysis both for the light they may cast on the shadowy domain of education production functions as well as on schooling equality.

These comments about the "improved schooling" hypothesis suggest that, while improved quality may be a necessary prerequisite for black economic advance, it was not the driving force in the rise in relative incomes. Demand side factors influencing the amount of discrimination "purchased" by whites seem to me to be a more important explanatory factor. There is some evidence for the significance of demand factors in explaining the sharp increase in black incomes in the 1960's. Regressions of black/white income or earnings ratios on various measures of federal antidiscrimination activity—such as Equal Employment Opportunities expenditures—yield highly significant coefficients.[2] E.E.O.C. and related post-1964 federal activity operated to increase the demand for blacks by penalizing discriminators and, in some instances, by pressing for "quota-type" employment practices. Omission of demand factors from Welch's analysis makes incomplete his picture of what has been going on in the market.

The possibility that the observed improvement in the relative status of the young is a temporary "starting position" phenomenon is often raised in discussion. Welch's evidence shows that "the relative value of schooling actually increased between 1959 and 1966 for three of four comparisons," contrary to the starting position or life-cycle explanation. Additional evidence regarding the likely persistence of income gains over time is shown in Table 1, where I summarize aggregate Census data on cohort incomes. In general, except for the 20-24 year old group, cohorts tend to preserve relative income ratios over time. These data do not, however, present as favorable a picture as Welch's 1959-1966 comparisons.

2. What are the implications of changed black-white income differentials for the education and labor markets? One striking impact of labor market improvements can already be observed in the education and career decisions of black students. Presumably as a result of the high rate of return to investments in education, the number of blacks

[2] *Black Elite*, Chapter 5.

TABLE 1

INCOME RATIOS BY CENSUS COHORTS

Cohort Age in 1949	Income Ratio, All Men		
	1949	1959	1969
20-24	.68	.68	.62
25-34	.59	.59	.57
35-44	.55	.55	.56
45-54	.54	.51	—
	Income Ratio, H.S. Graduates		
20-24	0.74	0.67	—
25-34	0.71	0.66	—
35-44	0.67	0.68	—
45-54	0.63	0.67	—
	Income Ratio, College Graduates		
20-24	0.81	0.70	—
25-34	0.67	0.66	—
35-44	0.59	0.53	—
45-54	0.56	0.44	—

SOURCE: U.S. Census of Population, 1950, Special Report: Education; U.S. Census of Population, 1960, Subject Report: Educational Attainment; Current Population Reports, Consumer Income, 1970.

enrolling in college increased greatly in the late 1960's. At the same time, the fields of study and career plans of black college men changed drastically, with a shift into "traditionally closed" areas such as accounting, business administration, and law. Regression calculations indicate that these shifts result from economically responsive supply behavior.[3]

To the extent that market discrimination depends critically on the absence of minority employers and skilled complementary workers, these shifts have a further implication for the future. As the supply of black managers and profes-

[3] See *Black Elite*, Chapter 3, or "The Implications of the Changing Labor Market for Minorities," in Kerr, *op. cit.*

sionals increases, opportunities for the less skilled to avoid discriminatory co-workers will increase and discrimination will decline in the market. The ultimate result of the improved economic status of the college-trained black may be the demise of discrimination throughout the market.

3. How should our theory of discrimination be revised in light of the new findings? Prior to the evidence given by the paper before us and in *Black Elite*, the principal fact to explain was the persistence and stability of black-white economic differences over long periods of time. What must be explained now is the sharp improvement in the black position in the past two decades or so—a decline in labor and education market discrimination—in contrast to the apparent stability in differentials in earlier periods of time. On the basis of Welch's paper an important role must be given to education market discrimination in this re-evaluation.

There are several ways in which the recent decline and past stability in racial differentials might be reconciled in a unified theoretic framework. One approach is to reconsider the meaning of past stability in differentials: how important was lack of education and physical capital in preventing the developments of nondiscriminatory black alternative economic structures? What was the role of the initial concentration of blacks in declining southern agriculture in counteracting competitive falls against discrimination? A second approach might be to stress the role of collective behavior and government activity in causing the sharp change in discrimination. In this regard discrimination in education by governmental agencies deserves special attention, as Welch properly tells us. If a conscious "exploitation" theory is applied, with governments as the agent of group behavior, the causal mechanism may be changed economic benefits of discrimination due to technological or market developments. My research on the school resources allocated to blacks and whites in the South points strongly to "conscious exploitation" following disfranchisement of blacks in the 1890's.[4] As Welch notes, Mississippi and other states altered their laws or constitutions to permit differential expenditures by race in this period. Once blacks were removed from political influence, however, the question necessarily arises: Why spend any public funds on their schooling? The "exploitation" argument calls attention to the role of blacks as a cooperating factor of production in the South and to the value of their schooling in raising the productivity and income of white-controlled resources.

At the same time, however, it is important to recognize that attribution of changes in discrimination to public activities (schooling, antidiscriminaton laws, etc.) does not provide a complete theory of discrimination. It is also necessary—though difficult—to explain governmental discrimination or antidiscriminatory policy changes. Why did the ratio of black to white school resources decline in the South? Why did the federal government step into the labor market so sharply?

Finally, a third approach is to stress the change in discrimination due to private changes in market demand. The factors involved here might include, first, the development of industries where nondiscriminators have a greater economic advantage—those with flat cost curves, for example —or second, income induced changes in white demands for discrimination, or, third, changes in attitudes.

In sum, there has been a sharp collapse in black/white economic differences which calls for a re-evaluation of the theory of discrimination. Welch's paper contributes to our understanding of one potentially important element in this change in the market. Further work is needed, however, to construct a new model of discrimination which is consistent with recent as well as past experience.

[4] See my "The Longterm Persistence of Black/White Economic Differences: The Role of Education?" unpublished paper, Department of Economics, University of Chicago.

Orley Ashenfelter   DISCRIMINATION
                              AND
                        TRADE UNIONS

Racial, sexist, and other prejudices filter through the institutions of the labor market before they are turned into the differences in wages or earnings that cannot be accounted for by differences in productive ability and that we label as discrimination. Economists typically avoid analyzing the nature and determinants of prejudice itself, and prefer to concentrate on analyses of the effects that various institutions have in exacerbating or mitigating the amount of discrimination that results from a given set and level of prejudices. It is unlikely that this preference stems wholly, or even largely, from any evidence that public policies designed to decrease discrimination are less likely to be successful in changing the former than the latter, but rather from the fact that the economist's tools are better equipment for convincing analyses of phenomena directly observable in the marketplace. This paper contains the results of a quantitative investigation into the effects of the presence of one such institution, trade unionism, on the extent of discrimination against black and female workers. The analysis is conventional in the sense that there is no attempt to explain the nature of prejudice or how it varies. Instead, interest centers on the observable differences in institutional settings and what effect they have on the ratio of black to white wages, assuming all the while that prejudices either do not vary or vary independently of institutional settings.

The first section of the paper defines the effect of unionism on the wages of blacks relative to whites and sketches a procedure for empirical analysis of this question. The sec-

88

ond section contains a discussion of the likely determinants of a union's policy regarding race; while the third, fourth, and fifth sections contain the basic empirical results and their interpretation. The last section contains a discussion of the implications of our analysis and empirical results.

1. AN EMPIRICAL FRAMEWORK

In order to make our discussion concrete we require a quantitative definition of what we mean by the effect of the presence of trade unionism on the wages of black workers relative to the wages of white workers. A useful way to approach this problem is to distinguish at a point in time between three separate, hypothetically observable, average wage rates that might exist in the economy for a given race-sex group. The first of these is the average observed wage rate of all *union* workers in that race-sex group. The second is the average observed wage rate of all *nonunion* workers in that race-sex group. The third is the average wage in that race-sex group that would be observed in the *absence of all unionism* in the economy. We will assume throughout that all average wage rates have been standardized for differences among groups in average skill levels, regardless of the race, sex, or unionization status of that group. Interest centers primarily on the effect of the presence of unionism on the average wage of all black workers as a proportion of the average wage of all white workers and the average wage of all white female workers as a proportion of the average wage of all white male workers. Although the empirical material below focuses on both of these issues, for expositional purposes we will frame our discussion here in terms of the former only, with the understanding that other groups are implicitly being discussed by analogy.

With the stage set in this way, we define the effect of the presence of unionism on the average black/white relative wage as the proportionate difference between the current average wage of blacks relative to whites and the average

89

wage of blacks relative to whites that would prevail in the absence of all unionism in the economy.[1] If, for example, the ratio of the average black wage to the average white wage were currently .60 (.62), and if it would be .62 (.60) in the absence of unionism, the effect of the presence of unionism would be to reduce (increase) the black/white wage ratio by .03[=(.60 — .62)/(.62)], or 3 percent, from what it would be in the absence of unionism. Since we cannot observe the black/white wage ratio in the absence of unionism, however, it is necessary to look more closely at this definition before we can give it operational content.

Now it is a relatively straightforward matter to show that, as we have defined it, the effect of the presence of unionism on the black/white wage ratio can be decomposed into three separate effects.[2] One of these effects is simply the difference between the fraction of the black work force that belongs to unions and the fraction of the white work force that belongs to unions. If a typical black worker gains just as much from belonging to a union as a white worker, then the crucial question is whether black workers are as likely as white workers to get into unions. A second determinant

[1] We may be more precise if we put this in symbols. Letting R_b and R_w represent the current average wages of blacks and whites, respectively, and R_b^c and R_w^c the average wages of blacks and whites that would exist in the absence of unionism, we define the effect of the presence of unionism on the black/white relative wage as $\Delta = [(R_b/R_w) - (R_b^c/R_w^c)]/(R_b^c/R_w^c)$.

[2] In symbols, let B and W represent the fractions of all black and white employees in the economy who belong to unions; let M_b represent the proportionate wage difference between black union and nonunion workers and M_w the proportionate wage difference between white union and nonunion workers; and let D_b represent the proportionate difference between the wage of nonunion black workers and the wage they would have in the absence of unionism, and similarly for D_w. Then the effect of the presence of unionism on the black/white wage ratio is approximately $\Delta^* = BM_b - WM_w + (D_b - D_w)$. This is discussed more fully in my "Racial Discrimination and Trade Unionism," *The Journal of Political Economy*, 80 (May/June 1972), 435-464.

of the overall effect of unionism on the black/white wage ratio is the difference in the size of the union/nonunion wage advantage for black workers compared to the size of the union/nonunion wage advantage for white workers. If, for example, the likelihood of a black worker being unionized does not differ from that of a white worker, then the crucial question is whether, once black workers are in unions, they gain as much from unionization as do white workers.

Though they may pose difficult measurement problems, each of these components of the effect of the presence of unionism on the black/white wage ratio is observable. A third determinant is not generally observable. This is the difference between blacks and whites in the effect of the presence of unionism in one part of the economy on the wages of the corresponding nonunion workers in the remainder of the economy. Since it will not be possible to *estimate* the size of this component of the effect of unionism on the black/white wage ratio, it is necessary to emphasize the possible importance of this factor. The presence of unionism in one part of the economy will generally change the wages of nonunion workers from what they would have been in the absence of unionism. If, as a result of unionism, for example, wages are higher in the union sector than they would be in the absence of unionism, then total employment in that sector may be reduced from what it would have been. At least some of those workers who would have been employed in the union sector will have to be employed in the nonunion sector, and this may result in wages in the nonunion sector being bid below what they would have been in the absence of unionism. Alternatively, the threat of unionism emanating from the unionized sector may induce some nonunion employers to buy off that threat by raising wages above what they would have been in the absence of unionism. In either case the presence of unionism in one part of the economy has affected wages in the other part. Whether these indirect effects of unionism have a larger or smaller effect on the wages of nonunion black workers or nonunion white workers cannot be determined. Of course, if these effects are relatively small, or if they do not differ much in their incidence as between black and white workers, they will not seriously affect our estimates of the effect of unionism on the black/white wage ratio.[3]

Before we turn to a more detailed analysis, it is interesting to ask whether this general framework allows us to put any bounds on the size of the effect of unionism on the black/white wage ratio, given the available knowledge of general union wage effects. It is easy to see that we can define such bounds, and that they imply that the effect of unionism on the black/white wage ratio is not likely to be very large in either direction. Suppose, for example, that the average wage of all union workers is 15 percent higher than the average wage of nonunion workers and that one-third of white male employees belong to unions.[4] Suppose also, as is contrary to fact, the extreme case where no black workers are in unions. Since one-third of the white work force would have had their wages raised by 15 percent, the overall average wage of black workers relative to white workers would have decreased by the proportion .05 ($= 1/3 \times .15$), or 5 percent. Given an overall ratio of the wage of black males to white males of .60 in the absence of unionism, even in this *extreme case* the black/white wage

---

[3] Even if neither of these conditions is satisfied, our estimates of the effect of unionism on the black/white wage ratio by sector will all be affected by the same proportion so long as labor supply curves are very elastic to each sector, and the incidence of threats of unionism does not differ by sector or race. This is true because highly elastic supply curves imply a fixed relationship among sectoral wage rates in the absence of unionism. Likewise, they imply the *same* fixed relationship among the nonunion wage rates in these sectors, and this implies similar proportionate changes in each sector. Thus, our sectoral estimates would still be good estimates of the effect of unionism on black/white wage ratios in one sector relative to another.

[4] These are approximately the results that H. Gregg Lewis reports in *Unionism and Relative Wages in the United States* (Chicago: University of Chicago Press, 1963).

ratio would decline to only .57 [= .60 — .05 (.60)] in the presence of unionism.[5]

2. UNION RACE POLICY

Most unions have at least implicit policies regarding race. Moreover, these policies seem heterogeneous to an outside observer, despite the show of unanimity that is displayed by the leadership of the largest federations. The espoused policies range from the open declarations of nepotism that have been associated with some of the unions in the building trades[6] to the strong attachments to, and support from, civil rights organizations that have been associated with some of the unions in the governmental sector.[7] If we assume that the policies of many of these unions reflect democratic decision-making, it is interesting to inquire as to the reasons for the observed differences in racial policy. One possible explanation, of course, is that the extent of prejudice among the (white) rank-and-file workers of these unions varies, and that such differences are the cause of different policies. This is obviously not a very attractive explanation, both because the observed racial policies appear to vary more than one would expect on this basis and because it does not open up much hope for the possibility of

[5] I hasten to add that knowledge of the effect of unionism on the black/white relative wage provides no information about the effect of unionism on the level of the wage of black or white workers. In the example above, the drop in the *ratio* of black to white wages could have resulted from decreases or increases in the absolute wage rates of both groups, so long as these wages did not change proportionately.

[6] See, as an example, the discussion of the United Association of Plumbers in Richard P. Nathan, *Jobs and Civil Rights* (Washington, D.C.:, U.S. Commission on Civil Rights, 1969), pp. 194-195.

[7] See, as an example, the discussion of the 1968 Memphis strike by the American Federation of State, County, and Municipal Employees in Ray Marshall and Arvil Van Adams, "Racial Negotiations—The Memphis Case," in W. E. Chalmers and G. W. Cormick, eds., *Racial Conflict and Negotiations* (Ann Arbor, Mich.: Institute of Labor and Industrial Relations, U. of Michigan, 1971), pp. 71-107.

falsification by a test involving observable variables. An alternative way to proceed is to hold the extent of prejudice constant and to inquire as to the effect of observable factors upon a union's racial policy. We follow this latter procedure here, with an eye toward any implications we may discover regarding differences in union racial policies and their impact on the black/white wage ratio.

Given the racial preferences of the white rank-and-file workers in a union's jurisdiction, that union's policy regarding race will presumably depend in large measure on the extent to which black workers make up a sizable fraction of the union's jurisdiction both prior and subsequent to unionization. This is true because effective unionization requires that the union enroll enough of the workers in firms with identical products that the demand for all union labor is not highly elastic.[8] Failure to organize extensively enough will result in the inability of the union to obtain higher wages and better working conditions for its members, which, after all, is its reason for existence. Now if black workers make up a sizable fraction of the workers in the labor markets that must be organized for a union to be effective, the union leadership (and, implicitly, the white rank-and-file) faces a choice. Since black workers are less likely to join or remain with the union unless offered, and accorded, relatively equal treatment, the leadership may choose either to offer such treatment and obtain a higher probability of organizing extensively or to organize without black workers. So long as black workers make up a sizable fraction of the union's jurisdiction, of course, the latter choice may well be tantamount to the choice of no union at all. Thus, where there is an effective union we should expect a more egalitarian (less discriminatory) race policy the larger the fraction of that union's jurisdiction that was made up of substitutable black workers prior to unionization.

[8] By effective unionization, I mean unionization that results in higher wages for a union of workers than would otherwise have been the case had these workers remained nonunion.

This single principle seems to go a long way toward explaining the history of union racial policies in the United States. On the one hand, it predicts that where racial animosities run high *and* where black workers are a large substitutable work force it is less likely that effective unions will be formed. The U.S. South fits both of these conditions, and this may be at least one of the reasons that white workers in the South remain nonunion even today.[9] On the other hand, it also predicts a positive correlation between the extent to which a union's race policy is relatively egalitarian and the extent to which blacks were represented in the union's jurisdiction prior to effective unionization. As it turns out, the empirical coincidence between these two factors is indeed very high. Among the building trade unions, for example, the bricklayers and the plasterers and cement finishers may be contrasted with the plumbers and pipefitters and the electrical workers. The former trades contained significant numbers of skilled black workers prior to unionization whereas the latter trades have been unionized since their inception simply because they are a result of a much later technology. As is well known, the former of these craft unions are also much less discriminatory than the latter.[10] Likewise, the relatively egalitarian policies followed by the Packinghouse Workers, the United Mine Workers, and many of the industrial unions that organized the mass production industries in the 1930's were undoubtedly due in large part to the sizable fractions of these unions' jurisdictions that were composed of black workers prior to unionization.[11] Finally, even the earliest history of

[9] For a quantitative assessment of the importance of this issue see Ray Marshall, *The Negro and Organized Labor* (New York: John Wiley and Sons, 1965), pp. 196-202.

[10] For a detailed discussion see Herbert Northrup, *Organized Labor and the Negro* (New York: Harper and Brothers, 1944), pp. 43-44.

[11] See Walter A. Fogel, *The Negro in the Meat Industry* (Philadelphia: University of Pennsylvania Wharton School of Finance and Commerce, 1970), pp. 67-73, for a good discussion of the case in meatpacking, for example.

the American Federation of Labor is consistent with this general principle. Although Samuel Gompers and the leadership of the AFL initially argued for extensive organization of black workers so as to increase the size of the AFL rank and file, this policy was short lived. Since the AFL was a loose federation that depended on the affiliation of autonomous unions for its growth and survival, it became necessary to accommodate itself to the demands of constituent unions that did not share Gompers' original ideas if it was to continue its growth.[12]

A second important determinant of a union's policy regarding race is presumably the methods by which it seeks to affect wages and working conditions. At one *extreme* the union affects wages and conditions by exercising control of the supply of labor. Organization in this instance has historically followed the lines of a narrow skill grouping, both to keep the ratio of labor costs to total costs low in the union's jurisdiction and to maintain control of entrance to the skill. A natural *concomitant* of a discriminatory race policy in this situation is exclusion of blacks from the union and thus from employment in the union's jurisdiction. An important *result* of such exclusionary policies is the elimination of promotion possibilities for black workers within an industry organized on the basis of narrow crafts even when black workers make up a substantial fraction of the industry. At the other extreme the union affects wages and conditions solely through the use of a bargained settlement based on a strike threat. Organization in this instance must normally be all inclusive so as to insure the efficacy of a possible strike. A discriminatory race policy in this situation typically cannot result in direct union exclusion from employment because the hiring decision remains in the hands

[12] See the detailed discussion of this transformation in Herbert Hill, "The Racial Practices of Organized Labor—The Age of Gompers and After," in Arthur Ross and Herbert Hill (eds.), *Employment, Race, and Poverty* (New York: Harcourt, Brace and World, 1967), pp. 365-402; and also the discussion in Northrup, *op. cit.*, p. 8.

of the employer, and once hired a worker's support must be enlisted. So long as the union bargains over working conditions, however, it may be able to insist upon discriminatory treatment of black workers, particularly with respect to seniority and promotional possibilities.

As the preceding discussion indicates, it is not clear from the available evidence what aggregate effect the presence of unionism is likely to have had on the wages of blacks relative to whites. Nevertheless, the discussion does suggest the hypothesis that industrial unions are likely to be less discriminatory (more egalitarian) than craft unions.[13] First, the fraction of blacks in the jurisdictions of industrial unions both prior and subsequent to unionization has typically been much larger than in the case of craft unions. As we have seen, this generally implies a more egalitarian race policy. Second, craft unions tend to have greater control of the supply of labor and the hiring process than do industrial unions, and this also will tend to make them more discriminatory. We will turn to the evidence below, therefore, with an eye toward testing this hypothesis.

3. THE EXTENT OF UNIONIZATION

As we observed in the first section, one crucial determinant of the effect of the presence of unionism on the black/white or male/female wage ratio is the extent of unionization of black and female workers relative to white male workers. Until very recently detailed information on the distribution of unionization by race or sex was virtually nonexistent. Fortunately, this problem has been remedied somewhat in recent years because of the 1967 Survey of Economic Opportunity, an expanded version of the Current Population Survey that both over-sampled in low income

[13] As is well known, the terms "craft" and "industrial" as applied in this context are not strictly appropriate. A term better than "craft" union might be "referral" union, so as to signify appropriately that the union typically has some connection with the hiring process.

areas and included a question on union membership. Table 1 contains estimates from this source of the percentage of the employees in each of four race-sex groups who belonged to unions. These are undoubtedly the best estimates of the racial distribution of the extent of unionization that will be available for some time, unless a question on union membership is someday included in a general population census. The major disadvantage of these data is that union membership was not determined for government employees, so that the data we will discuss refer only to *private* wage and salary workers.[14]

TABLE 1

Percentage of Private Wage and Salary Workers Belonging to Unions, 1967, by Aggregate Occupation, Race and Sex

OCCUPATION GROUP	RACE-SEX GROUP			
	White Males	Black Males	White Females	Black Females
Blue-Collar Workers	42.7	36.1	22.5	22.3
Sales Workers	7.0	39.0	7.0	16.0
Clerical Workers	23.0	36.0	8.0	21.0
Managerial Workers	9.0	29.0	4.0	0.0
Professional Workers	11.0	16.0	4.0	10.0
All Workers	31.0	32.0	12.0	13.0

SOURCE: See Table 2.

[14] The only other source of data on the racial composition of union membership of which I am aware is the University of Michigan Survey Research Center's annual Survey of Consumer Finances, which does include a question on union membership. The sample size of the SCF is much smaller than that of the SEO, so that the information

The most striking impression given by Table 1 is the remarkable similarity in the extent of unionization of the black and white work forces. About 31 percent of white male workers belong to unions, which is nearly identical to the 32 percent of black male workers in unions. As can be seen from Table 1, this result is a combination of a slightly lower extent of unionization among black workers than among white workers in the blue-collar occupations, but a slightly higher extent of unionization for the former in the white-collar occupations. These differences are not, however, very substantial.

The second most striking impression from Table 1 is the very large discrepancy between the extent of unionization of male and female workers. Whereas 31 to 32 percent of male workers are union members, only 12 to 13 percent of female workers are union members. Moreover, the differences between men and women in extent of unionization exist in virtually every occupation group, including the white-collar occupations.

Perhaps to the surprise of some, these data do not paint the overall picture of a labor movement that is strongly exclusionary on the basis of race. To some extent the roughly equal unionization figures for blacks and whites may simply reflect a number of offsetting demographic and geographic characteristics of the two work forces. On the one hand, for example, the extent of unionization tends to be low in the South, which is the home of a disproportionately large number of black workers. On the other hand, the extent of unionization tends to be high in urban areas, and these are also the home of a disproportionately large number of black workers.

---

from it does not give the detail presented here. I have, however, compared the estimates of extent of unionization by race and occupation from the two sets of data, and they are very similar. I am indebted to Professor George Johnson of the University of Michigan for making the SCF data available for the comparison.

Since male blue-collar workers constitute the bulk of American unionists, Tables 2 and 3 contain a more detailed picture of the extent of unionization of white and black workers in this group. These data should shed some light on the hypothesis that craft unions are likely to be more exclusionary than industrial unions. Of the industries in the tables, only construction is organized solely along craft lines, so that this hypothesis predicts a significantly smaller extent of unionization of black workers relative to white workers in the construction industry than in the other industries in the tables. This clearly turns out to be the case for both craftsmen and operatives. Whereas well over one-half the white craftsmen in the building trades belong to unions, only about one-quarter of the black craftsmen in the building trades belong to unions, and the same discrepancy exists for operatives. Likewise, the extent of unionization of black and white craftsmen and operatives in the remainder of the industry groups in Tables 2 and 3 is very similar. For example, 44 percent of white nonconstruction craftsmen are unionized, while 46 percent of blacks in this group are unionized. For nonconstruction operatives the comparable figures are: white workers 48 percent, and black workers 45 percent. We conclude, therefore, that the craft-dominated building trades unions show a much smaller extent of unionization of black workers relative to white workers than is true in the industrially organized sector. This is strong evidence in support of the hypothesis that craft unions are more discriminatory than industrial unions.

In sum, we observe a similar extent of unionization of black and white male workers in nonconstruction industries and among construction laborers. We also observe a significantly smaller extent of unionization of skilled black workers than of skilled white workers in construction. Finally, taken together with a significantly greater level of unionization among black white-collar workers, we observe that the overall extent of unionization of black and white male workers is virtually identical.

100

TABLE 2

Percentage of White Male Blue-Collar Private Wage and Salary Workers Belonging to Unions, 1967, by Occupation and Industry

OCCUPATION GROUP	ALL INDUSTRIES	SELECTED MAJOR INDUSTRIES				
		Construction	Durable Manufacturing	Nondurable Manufacturing	Transportation, Communication, Utilities	Wholesale and Retail Trade
Craftsmen	47.	53.9	53.2	48.3	66.9	16.3
Operatives	48.	53.4	57.6	47.2	65.1	18.6
Laborers	30.	28.2	51.0	48.8	59.7	16.8
Service Workers	19.	N.A.[a]	29.5	41.6	N.A.[a]	12.0

SOURCES: These data are derived from the 1967 Survey of Economic Opportunity. Since this survey is especially supplemented by a relatively unique sampling design, estimates of population proportions such as these must be computed by weighting individuals by estimated probabilities of being sampled. See, for example, the discussion in U.S. Bureau of the Census, *Current Population Reports*, series P-20, No. 216, "Labor Union Membership in 1966." I owe a debt of gratitude to Professor Daniel Saks of Michigan State University for providing me with these calculations during his stay at The Brookings Institution.

[a] Not available because too few employees in the sample were in this category.

TABLE 3

Percentage of Black Male Blue-Collar Private Wage and Salary Workers Belonging to Unions, 1967, by Occupation and Industry

OCCUPATION GROUP	ALL INDUSTRIES	SELECTED MAJOR INDUSTRIES				
		Construction	Durable Manufacturing	Nondurable Manufacturing	Transportation, Communication, Utilities	Wholesale and Retail Trade
Craftsmen	40.	26.9	67.6	40.5	62.7	20.3
Operatives	44.	21.5	64.5	39.3	62.1	14.2
Laborers	33.	35.1	49.6	35.3	56.1	14.7
Service Workers	19.	N.A.	47.3	30.3	N.A.	11.3

SOURCES: See Table 2.

4. UNION/NONUNION WAGE DIFFERENTIALS

As we also pointed out in the first section, a second crucial determinant of the magnitude of the effect of the presence of unionization on black/white and female/male wage ratios is the differential between union and nonunion average wage rates and whether this differential varies as between race-sex groups. Holding constant the likelihood of being in a union, for example, how large a wage advantage does a black worker gain from being in a union and is this advantage greater or smaller than would accrue to a similarly placed white worker?

Table 4 contains estimates for male workers of the proportionate difference between the hourly wage rates of union and nonunion workers from the same source as the data in Tables 1 through 3. Differences between union and nonunion workers in education, experience, and many other characteristics that might be associated with wage rates have been controlled so as to make these comparisons a skill-corrected set. Thus, the union and nonunion workers that we are comparing are statistically as similar as we can make them. The results in Table 4 are collapsed somewhat, in terms of the number of industry groups for which union/nonunion differentials are reported, only because initial calculations showed remarkably similar union/nonunion wage differentials for all of the nonconstruction industry groups.[15]

The most striking impression given by Table 4 is the very significant difference for both race groups between union/nonunion wage differentials of blue-collar workers in the construction industry as compared to union/nonunion wage differentials of blue-collar workers in all other industries. The average union wage exceeds the average nonunion wage by at least 30 percent in each occupation group in the construction industry for *both* black and white workers,

[15] For a report of these more detailed results see Orley Ashenfelter, *op. cit.*

TABLE 4

Estimates of Proportionate (in logs) Union/Nonunion Wage Differentials by Occupation for Males[a]

OCCUPATION	WHITE WORKERS		BLACK WORKERS	
	Noncon-struction	Con-struction	Noncon-struction	Con-struction
Craftsmen	.027	.333	.118	.416
	(.022)	(.035)	(.035)	(.056)
Operatives	.142	.362	.197	.285
	(.020)	(.086)	(.023)	(.094)
Laborers	.177	.390	.274	.377
	(.044)	(.075)	(.032)	(.049)
	ALL INDUSTRIES		ALL INDUSTRIES	
Professional Workers	.120		.282	
	(.046)		(.120)	
Managerial Workers	.006		—.116	
	(.050)		(.112)	
Clerical Workers	.018		.112	
	(.041)		(.049)	
Sales Workers	—.007		.275	
	(.064)		(.093)	
Service Workers	.034		.165	
	(.050)		(.038)	

SOURCE: See text.

[a] Estimated standard errors of estimated coefficients are enclosed in parentheses.

and it is significantly higher than 30 percent in most of these building trades occupations. On the other hand, the average union wage exceeds the average nonunion wage by only about 10 percent for the total of the blue-collar workers in other industries. Second, in the building trades occupations there is no strong relationship between skill level and the size of union/nonunion wage differentials, with differentials approximately the same in each of the occupation groups. On the other hand, there is a strong inverse correlation between the size of union/nonunion wage differentials and skill level in all other industries. The average wage of unionized nonconstruction craftsmen, for example, is 2.7 percent higher than the average wage of comparable nonunion workers; but the average wages of unionized nonconstruction operatives and laborers are 14.2 percent and 17.7 percent higher than comparable nonunion workers. Third, although union/nonunion wage differentials are very similar for both black and white workers in the construction sector, they are higher for black workers than for white workers in all but one of the other occupation-industry categories listed in Table 4. This, of course, is additional strong evidence for the hypothesis that craft unions are likely to be more discriminatory than industrial unions.

Finally, I have brought together the estimated union/nonunion wage differentials by race and sex in Table 5. As

TABLE 5

Overall Estimates of Percentage Union/Nonunion Wage Differentials by Race and Sex, 1967

White Males	Black Males	White Females	Black Females
9.7	20.5	15.0	7.2

can be seen from the table, the estimated differentials are higher for both white females and black males than for white males, while the estimated differential for black females is lower than all of the preceding three. Taken together these results imply that, if they get into unions, both black males and white females gain higher wage advantages than do white males. As we have seen, the larger wage advantage for black males than for white males results solely from higher wage advantages in nonconstruction industries.

105

These results contain only a part of the story, however, until they have been coupled with the extent of unionization data presented in Section 3 to produce estimates of the overall effect of the presence of unionization on the black/white and female/male wage ratios. We therefore turn to these results in the next section.

5. THE OVERALL EFFECTS OF THE PRESENCE OF UNIONISM

Recall that we have defined the effect of the presence of unionism on the black/white wage ratio as the proportionate difference between the current ratio of black to white wages and what we estimate that ratio would be in the absence of unionism. As we have seen, the size of this effect depends on the differences in the extent of unionization between blacks and whites that we reported in Section 3, and the differences in union/nonunion wage differentials reported in Table 4. As it turns out, the fact that the estimated union/nonunion wage differentials in this latter table vary inversely with skill level for both black and white workers implies that the overall effect of unionism on the black/white wage ratio will also depend on the distribution of black and white workers by skill level. For this reason Table 6 contains estimates of the fraction of the total wages and salaries received by black and white male workers in each occupation and industry listed in Table 4. Thus, for example, 18.0 percent of the total wage and salary dollars received by white male workers per hour was received by workers who were craftsmen in the nonconstruction industries. The compensation distribution in Table 6 is similar to a conventional occupational distribution, except that each occupational category has been weighted by its economic importance, where the latter is measured by its average wage rate.[16]

[16] Instead of .180 being the probability that a white male worker

TABLE 6

Estimates of the Proportion of Total Compensation of Private Wage and Salary Workers Received by Occupational Groups for Males

OCCUPATION	WHITE WORKERS		BLACK WORKERS	
	Noncon-struction	Con-struction	Noncon-struction	Con-struction
Craftsmen	.180	.073	.106	.048
Operatives	.208	.010	.325	.013
Laborers	.048	.015	.144	.070

	ALL INDUSTRIES	ALL INDUSTRIES
Professional Workers	.147	.041
Managerial Workers	.134	.014
Clerical Workers	.065	.062
Sales Workers	.069	.012
Service Workers	.036	.112
Private Household Workers	.001	.001
Farm Workers	.014	.054

SOURCE: These estimates are obtained by weighting employment by mean wage rate for each category and then deflating by the sum of these quantities. Employment estimates and mean wage rates are from the 1967 Survey of Economic Opportunity (see the notes to Table 2).

Combining the results in Section 3 with the data in Tables 4 and 5 gives the overall effects of unionization on black/white and female/male wage ratios that are given in Table 7.[17] First, as the table shows, the effect of unionism

---

is a nonconstruction craftsman, it is the probability that a dollar from a white male worker was earned by a nonconstruction craftsman.

[17] These estimates are obtained as $\triangle = \Sigma E_{bi} M_{bi} B_i - \Sigma E_{wi} M_{wi} W_i$ where the E_{bi} and the E_{wi} are the entries in Table 6, the M_{bi} and M_{wi} are the entries in Table 4, and the B_i and W_i are aggregations from

TABLE 7

Estimates of the Effect of Unionism on the Average Wage of
Black and Female Workers Relative to White Male Workers

Difference Between:	
Black Male Workers and White Male Workers in	
(1) Construction: Blue-Collar Occupations	—.050
(2) Non-Construction: Blue-Collar Occupations	.039
(3) White-Collar Occupations	.026
(4) All Workers	.034
White Female Workers and White Male Workers	—.019
Black Female Workers and White Male Workers	—.028
All Black Workers and All White Workers	.017

in the building construction trades is to lower the ratio of
black to white male wages by about 5 percent in those
trades. As we have seen, this does not result from differences in the wage advantage of black workers once they are
in one of these unions, but from the fact that the likelihood
of a black worker in the building trades gaining access to
a union job is less than half the likelihood of a white worker
gaining access to such a job. Second, the effect of unionism
in the nonconstruction blue-collar occupations is to raise the
ratio of black to white male wages by about 3.9 percent in
those occupations. This positive effect does not result from
differences in the extent of unionization of black and white
workers in these occupations. Rather, it results from the
fact that (i) within each of these occupations the union/
nonunion wage advantage is greater for black workers than
for white workers, *and* (ii) black workers tend to be disproportionately concentrated in those occupations where
union/nonunion wage advantages are greatest for both
black and white workers. Taken together with the positive

Tables 1, 2, and 3. See Orley Ashenfelter, *op. cit.*, for the more technical details, and comparable estimates from other data sources.

effect of unionism on the black/white wage ratio in white-collar occupations, these results imply that the overall effect of the presence of unionism is to raise the black/white wage ratio for male workers by about 3.4 percent.

Finally, the effect of unionism is to reduce the ratio of white female wages to white male wages by 1.9 percent, and to reduce the ratio of black female wages to white male wages by 2.8 percent. As we have seen, the main reason for this negative effect of unionism on the female/male wage ratio is that female workers are only about one-third as likely as male workers to belong to unions. The combined effect of unionism on the wages of males and females implies that the ratio of black to white wages of all workers might have been 1.7 percent higher in 1967 than it would have been in the absence of all unionism.

6. CONCLUSIONS AND IMPLICATIONS

In this paper we have examined the question of whether the presence of trade unionism in the American economy exacerbates or mitigates the extent of labor market discrimination against black and female workers. It is important to stress that none of our findings implies that most, or indeed any, American trade unions do not discriminate against black workers. We simply ask whether there is more or less discrimination against black and female workers in the average unionized labor market or in the average nonunion labor market, but not whether discrimination is entirely absent from either. With this limitation in mind the following concluding remarks seem appropriate.

First, on an empirical level we consistently find a higher ratio of black to white wages in labor markets organized by industrial unions than in unorganized labor markets. We also consistently find that the ratio of black to white wages in labor markets organized by craft or "referral" unions differs little from that ratio in unorganized labor markets. At the same time we find that the proportion of black workers who are unionized differs little from the proportion of white workers who are unionized in the industrial union sector, but that the former is about one-half the latter in the craft union sector. Under certain simplifying assumptions these results taken together imply that in 1967 the ratio of black to white male wages might have been 4 percent higher in the industrial union sector and 5 percent lower in the craft union sector than they would have been in the absence of all unionism. The average of these two effects is positive, however, so that the ratio of black to white male wages may have been some 3.4 percent higher in 1967 than it would have been in the absence of unionism. Combining the effect of the presence of unionism on the wages of black males relative to white males with its effect on the wages of black females relative to white females suggests that the ratio of the wages of *all* black workers relative to *all* white workers might have been 1.7 percent higher in 1967 than it would have been in the absence of unionism. Finally, comparable estimates for female workers imply that the ratio of white female to white male wages might have been 1.9 percent lower than they would have been in the absence of unionism.

Second, the most important conclusion that I draw from these results does not, in fact, concern their sign, but their magnitude. All in all, they suggest to me that the presence of trade unionism is not a major factor affecting wage differentials between black and white workers or between male and female workers. For example, the hourly wage of black male workers was a little greater than 70 percent of the hourly wage of white male workers in 1967. Thus, the male black/white wage ratio would have to increase by roughly 45 percent to bring black and white wages into equality. According to our results above, the presence of unionism may have increased the male black/white wage ratio by as much as 4 percent, which is less than one-tenth of the change that would be required for complete equality. Even if the sign of our effect were somehow incorrect, the

110

basic point would remain. When compared with the size of the overall gap in hourly wages between black and white or male and female workers, the effect of unionism does not appear to be very important.

Finally, these results have implications for some specific areas of public policy. To begin with, they imply that efforts to combat discrimination by unions in the building trades are likely to have a greater payoff to black workers than are efforts in other sectors. This is true both because the presence of unionism in the building trades reduces the black/white wage ratio there, *and* because this is accomplished primarily by excluding black workers *who are already in the building trades* from access to union membership. Of course, whether greater resources should actually be devoted by private and public agencies to fighting discrimination in this sector than in others also requires an assessment of the relative costs of so doing. This also raises the issue of the general strategy that should be followed by private and public civil rights organizations in dealing with discrimination in the craft sector. One strategy, which is clearly being followed even today by some activists, is to try to get black workers into the building trades unions, using any of a large number of tactics. As we have seen, black workers who get into unions in this sector do gain very significant wage advantages, and these are not much different from the wage advantages of white workers who get into these unions. In a sense, the existence of unionism in the building trades results in a pot of gold that may be distributed arbitrarily among workers. Given that this pot of gold exists, it seems only equitable that black workers should receive their share of it, and such a position essentially implies a strategy that calls for efforts to get black workers admitted to these unions. A second and far more radical strategy, of course, would involve an effort to weaken significantly the building trades unions. This could result either in a significant reduction in the extent of unionism of white workers in these trades or in a reduction of the already very large wage dif-

111

ferentials that accrue to unionized building trades workers. Efforts to suspend or repeal the Davis-Bacon Act could be one part of such a strategy, for example. If one were interested strictly in efficient resource allocation, the second of these strategies would clearly be preferable. From the point of view of increasing the total income that accrues to the black community, however, I suspect that the first of these strategies may be preferable. The choice between them, therefore, is likely to depend in part on one's judgments regarding the equity versus efficiency issues involved. If it turns out that a strategy based on significantly increasing the extent of unionization of black workers in the building trades is unsuccessful, it would not be surprising to find a new and somewhat unusual conjunction of interest groups that were determined to weaken significantly the strength of many of the craft unions in the United States.

Herbert Hill   COMMENT

Professor Ashenfelter's paper is largely devoted to show-
ing that craft unions lower the wages of blacks relative to
whites as compared to the ratio in nonunion markets, and
that industrial unions raise the wages of blacks relative to
whites as compared to the ratio in nonunion markets. However, the paper does not show that industrial unions also
discriminate against black workers. Because readers might
get the erroneous impression from the paper that industrial
unions do not discriminate, I shall use my comment to review some of the relevant evidence that they do.

A significant feature of the development of case law under Title VII of the Civil Rights Act of 1964 is that few judicial decisions concerned with substantive issues have been
rendered in cases in which the employer is the sole de-
fendant. The most important cases decided under Title VII
have included both employers and labor unions, or unions
and labor-management apprenticeship committees, as joint
defendants. Since virtually all facets of employment in unionized industries are regulated, although not uniformly,
by both employers and labor unions, it has become necessary to join them both as respondents in charges before the
Equal Employment Opportunity Commission and in law-
suits under Title VII. The federal courts have come to realize that in unionized industries both parties share responsibility for whatever forms of racial discrimination exist and
have recognized the necessity of naming as co-defendants
both parties to the collective bargaining agreement in order
to eliminate discriminatory patterns and to grant adequate
remedies. This is especially so if the issue involves questions
of seniority and job assignment.[1]

[1] See Herbert Hill, "The New Judicial Perception of Employment

In *U.S.* v. *Hayes International Corp.*,[2] the government filed suit against the company exclusively, but the court ordered it to join the collective bargaining representative, Local 1155 of the United Automobile, Aerospace and Agricultural Implement Workers of America (UAW), as a necessary party to the litigation. The court decision emphasized that "This court has previously held that in Title VII cases bringing into issue seniority, promotions and similar matters, the union should be enjoined. . . ."[3] This has become a standard practice of the federal courts and of the Equal Employment Opportunity Commission.

Now that the courts have repeatedly found a variety of discriminatory seniority systems and job assignment practices to be unlawful and have ordered far-reaching revisions of these practices, unions operating in diverse jurisdictions have increasingly persisted in extensive efforts to prevent change in racial patterns.[4] There are real, but nonetheless self-generated reasons for the adamant resistance of labor unions to the requirements of contemporary civil

---

Discrimination: Litigation Under Title VII of the Civil Rights Act of 1964," *University of Colorado Law Review*, 43, No. 3 (March 1972), 243-268.

[2] U.S. v. Hayes International Corp., 294 F. Supp. 803 (N.D. Ala., 1968); rev'd and rem'd 415 F. 2nd 1038 (5th Cir., 1969); decision on remand part —F. 2d—, 4 EPD para. 7690 (5th Cir., 1971).

[3] *Ibid.*

[4] Among the cases involving discrimination in job assignment and seniority, see United States v. Bethlehem Steel Corp., 446 F. 2d 652 (2nd Cir., 1971); Quarles v. Philip Morris, Inc., 279 F. Supp. 505 (E.D. Va. 1968); United States v. Local 189, Paper Workers (Crown Zellerbach Corp.), 282 F. Supp. 39 (E.D. La. 1968) (preliminary order), 301 F. Supp. 906 (1969) (final order), aff'd, 416 F. 2d 980 (5th Cir., 1969), cert. denied, 397 U.S. 919 (1970). See also Taylor v. Armco Steel, 429 F. 2d 498 (5th Cir., 1970); Hicks v. Crown Zellerbach Corp., 319 F. Supp. 314 (E.D. La. 1970); Long v. Georgia Kraft Co., 328 F. Supp. 681 (N.D. Ga. 1970); Robinson v. P. Lorillard Co., 319 F. Supp. 835 (M.D.N.C. 1970), aff'd in part, rev'd in part, 3 CCH Emp. Prac. Dec. para. 8267 (4th Cir., 1971); United States v. Continental Can Co., 319 F. Supp. 161 (E.D. Va. 1970).

rights laws and judicial decisions. In many sectors of the economy, organized labor created racial job patterns in the past that have become institutionalized through the structure of collective bargaining. For generations, black workers were systematically excluded from entering certain departments and seniority lines of progression leading to the most desirable jobs.

Seniority systems are designed to provide some order and structure in the method of selecting employees for promotion and layoff. But an employee's seniority status is essentially a firm expectation that under certain conditions—notably in the matter of promotion, furlough, and dismissal—his future employment status is regulated and determined by standards defined in relation to other workers, which are codified in the collective bargaining agreement. Court decisions ordering broad changes in seniority systems and job assignment practices that are found to discriminate have imperiled the heretofore legally sanctioned expectations of white workers, which have been based upon the systematic denial of the job rights of black workers. Attempts to ward off judicial interference in seniority arrangements on the grounds that it will anger and frustrate the "legitimate" and "hard-earned" expectations of white employees who individually are not responsible for the origin and perpetuation of patterns of racial discrimination have been rejected by the courts.

The earliest cases involving seniority provisions in union contracts in which the Equal Employment Opportunity Commission filed briefs *amicus curiae* were *Quarles* v. *Philip Morris Company*[5] and *Hicks* v. *Crown Zellerbach Corporation.*[6] In these cases the courts for the first time in American jurisprudence specifically restructured the provisions of a collective bargaining agreement to eliminate unlawful racial practices and to give black workers equal employ-

[5] Quarles v. Philip Morris, Inc., 279 F. Supp. 505 (E.D. Va. 1968).
[6] Hicks v. Crown Zellerbach Corp., 321 F. Supp. 1241 (E.D. La. 1971).

ment opportunities. In *Quarles*, the court held that seniority is not a vested interest and was subject to change.

A major example of labor resistance to Title VII requirements is to be found in the response of the United Steelworkers of America (AFL-CIO), a major industrial union. In 1970, after many years of protest by black steel workers, a federal court found the Steelworkers Union and the Bethlehem Steel Corporation in Lackawanna, New York, to be in violation of the law. In *United States* v. *Bethlehem Steel Corp.*, the court stated:

> The pervasiveness and longevity of the overt discriminatory hiring and job assignment practices, admitted by Bethlehem and the unions, compel the conclusion that the present seniority and transfer provisions were based on past discriminatory classifications. . . . Job assignment practices were reprehensible. Over 80 percent of black workers were placed in eleven departments which contained the hotter and dirtier jobs in the plant. Blacks were excluded from higher paying and cleaner jobs.[7]

The court observed that discriminatory contract provisions were embodied in nationwide master agreements negotiated by the international union in 1962, 1965, and 1968. The court also stated that:

> The Lackawanna plant was a microcosm of classic job discrimination in the North, making clear why Congress enacted Title VII of the Civil Rights Act of 1964.[8]

On October 14, 1971, the court issued a decree defining as members of the affected class some 1600 black steelworkers (members of the union), who were entitled to receive benefits as a result of the court's decision. It is significant to note that in the *Bethlehem Steel* case, the Court of Appeals for the Second Circuit stated:

[7] U.S. v. Bethlehem Steel Corp., 446 F. 2d 652 (2nd Cir., 1971).
[8] *Ibid.*

Appellees also argue that the morale of employees who did not suffer discrimination will suffer if rate retention and seniority carryover are ordered. But in the context of this case that possibility is not such an overriding business purpose that the relief requested must be denied. Assuming *arguendo* that the expectations of some employees will not be met, their hopes arise from an illegal system.[9]

The court of appeals continued with a statement on the expectations of employees who benefited from provisions of collective bargaining agreements by virtue of depriving other employees who did not benefit from such agreements:

Moreover, their seniority advantages are not indefeasibly vested rights but mere expectations derived from a bargaining agreement subject to modification. . . . If relief under Title VII can be denied merely because the majority group of employees, who have not suffered discrimination, will be unhappy about it, there will be little hope of correcting the wrongs to which the Act is directed.[10]

In *Robinson v. Lorillard Corporation,* the Fourth Circuit Court of Appeals stated:

We recognize Lorillard's point that changing the minority system may frustrate the expectations of employees who have established departmental seniority in the preferable departments. However, Title VII guarantees that all employees are entitled to the same expectations regardless of "race, color, religion, sex or national origin." *Where some employees now have lower expectations than their co-workers because of the influence of one of these foreladen factors, they are entitled to have their expectations raised even if the expectations of others must be lowered in order to achieve the statutorily mandated equality of opportunity.* (Emphasis added.)[11]

[9] *Ibid.*   [10] *Ibid.*
[11] Robinson v. Lorillard Corp., 444 F. 2d 791 (4th Cir., 1971).

117

All of the federal court cases under Title VII dealing with the racial consequences of union-negotiated seniority systems have brought the case law into unanimity. Decisions in such cases as *Quarles, Crown Zellerbach, Taylor* v. *Armco Steel,*[12] *Robinson* v. *Lorillard,* and *U.S.* v. *Bethlehem Steel* have rejected considerations of the employment expectations of white employees when it has been shown that the expectations of black employees involving job advancement, higher working levels, the development of greater skills, increased wages and job security have been frustrated by racial discrimination over a period of many years.

Racial exclusion practices by labor organizations that deny black workers union membership and employment, as in the building trades and other craft unions, are only one aspect of discrimination by organized labor. In contrast to the craft unions, which exclude blacks from membership, the industrial unions do organize black workers but often discriminate against them in several ways after they have been admitted to the union. The discriminatory practices of the industrial unions have significant consequences for black workers and members of other minority groups.

Frequently these unions fail to provide "fair representation" to nonwhite members and refuse to process their grievances.[13] The use of new testing devices and other non-work-related qualifications, although nondiscriminatory on their face, keep black workers out of desirable jobs just as effectively as the "white only" clauses did in the past. Segregated seniority and job assignment provisions in union contracts which were once openly labeled "white" and "colored" have been eliminated; but separate lines of pro-

---

[12] Taylor v. Armco Steel Corp., 2 EPD para. 10,024 Southern District, Texas, 1969, reversed and remanded 429 F. 2d 498 (5th Cir., 1970).

[13] Among the cases involving racial aspects of the duty of fair representation, see NLRB v. Local 12, Rubber Workers, 368 F. 2d 12 (5th Cir., 1966), cert. denied, 389 U.S. 837 (1967); Master Stevedores Ass'n, 156 NLRB 78 (1966); Independent Metal Workers, 147 NLRB 1573 (1964); Goodyear Tire & Rubber Co., 45 Lab. Arb. 240 (1965).

motion are maintained in more subtle ways. The wording has changed, but the consequences for black workers are the same. Industrial unions also frequently prevent the equal participation of nonwhites in leadership positions.[14]

As black workers in the steel industry, in pulp and paper manufacturing, in oil and chemical refineries, in tobacco factories and other industries have learned, what exclusion is to the craft unions, separate lines of job promotion and seniority are to the industrial unions. Although these practices are illegal, many industrial unions continue to negotiate discriminatory racial seniority systems in collective bargaining agreements, and vigorously defend their traditional racial practices.

The many findings of the Equal Employment Opportunity Commission and decisions of the courts reveal that the policies of craft unions which exclude blacks and of industrial unions which discriminate after membership has been granted to black workers constitute a difference of form rather than of substance.

The impact on employees of seniority procedures and job assignment practices was noted by the United States Supreme Court in its decision in *Humphrey* v. *Moore*: "Seniority has become of overriding importance and one of its major functions is to determine who gets or who keeps an available job."[15]

By the 1940's the majority of labor unions affiliated with the American Federation of Labor had settled into a policy of racial exclusion or segregation. In various industries, organized labor established segregated locals or all-black auxiliary units, excluded black workers from certain job classifications, and created separate racial seniority and promotional lines in union contracts. And, finally, in many crafts they refused to organize black labor.

[14] See H. Hill, "Black Dissent in Organized Labor" in J. Boskin and R. Rosenstone (eds.), *Seasons of Rebellion: Protest and Radicalism in Recent America* (New York: Holt, Rinehart and Winston, 1972), pp. 55-80.

[15] Humphrey v. Moore, 375 U.S. 335 (1964).

These and other practices made possible the greater exploitation of black workers, as a means of subsidizing the wages of white workers. The overall policy of discriminating against black workers has lowered total labor costs because the employer of blacks could trade off higher wages for white workers against the wages of lower-paid blacks.

This pattern continues into the 1970's and is the legacy of a joint labor-management tradition. For example, in most steelmills, the millwright is white and the millwright's helper is black. They do substantially the same work; in fact, the black helper usually teaches the job skills to the white millwright, who receives higher pay and has a higher job classification. Many examples of this pattern can be cited in other industries. Apart from its consequences to organized labor, employers of blacks derive substantial benefits from a labor policy that results in lower average costs.

White workers benefit from this deprivation of blacks, which subsidizes higher wages and working conditions for whites, individually and as a class. Discriminatory unions and segregated seniority and promotional lines in labor agreements have directly contributed to this process. In reality, employment discrimination, either as total exclusion of blacks from a craft or as limitation to inferior classification, has been a form of subsidization to the white worker and his union. Thus, organized labor and employers have jointly created a highly exploited class of black labor, rigidly blocked from advancing into the all-white occupations. The white electrician, by virtue of the exclusion of blacks from the trade, does not have to compete with an entire class within the working population. This also perpetuates the white—that is, high status—of the craft occupation. In this way, "white" and "high status" are synonymous and interdependent. In certain desirable occupations in industrial plants, white workers are also exempted from competition with blacks; they are assigned classifications which have a higher wage base (supported by the payment of lower

120

wages to blacks) and have access to better-paying, more skilled jobs not open to blacks.

As a result, white workers have expectations of both the opportunity for earnings and promotion which are based in varying degrees on the denial of equal opportunity to blacks. The elimination of racial employment inequality necessarily affects the expectations of white workers, since it compels competition with black workers where none previously existed. White worker expectations have become the norm; thus, when racial practices that have historically disadvantaged blacks are removed to eliminate the present effects of past discrimination, whites believe that preferential treatment is given to blacks. It is, in fact, the removal of the preferential treatment traditionally enjoyed by white workers at the expense of black wage earners that is now at issue. These self-generated factors—the result of the historic dual labor system based on race—account for the *maximum resistance* by labor unions and employers to changes in the status of the black labor force.

The industrial unions of the Congress of Industrial Organizations arrived late on the scene. At the beginning of the new industrial union movement, in the mid-1930's, the CIO adopted a policy of formal racial equality. Although unevenly implemented and often ignored by its affiliates, the CIO's equalitarian program represented an important break with the AFL tradition. But under pressure from powerful AFL international unions (such as the injection of the racial issue in organizing campaigns and in "raiding" activities) and after the merger of the CIO with the AFL in 1955, the CIO's enlightened racial policies were, in many cases, replaced by the traditional racial practices of the major AFL affiliates.

By refusing to organize black workers in the first instance, labor unions permitted employers to exploit black workers who remained a vast unorganized portion of the labor force. At a later period, when industrial unionism re-

121

quired the inclusion of all employees in large collective bargaining units, the forms of discrimination changed. What had been informal discriminatory job patterns became more rigid when separate, racially based seniority and promotional lines were codified in collective bargaining contracts. In some mass production industries, the job mobility of black workers became even more limited after union organization.

After some initial skepticism based on their earlier experience with trade unions, black workers had come to accept the CIO. But by the mid-1950's they found that they had become the victims of a different kind of discriminatory pattern. Throughout the steel industry in the South, for example, where patterns of segregation had been casual, many more job classifications had been available to black workers before unionization imposed rigid and enforceable classifications and seniority systems in collective bargaining agreements which provided for job assignments on the basis of race. Blacks now began to protest the separate racial seniority lines. But once again, white union leaders traded off the rights of black workers to obtain greater benefits for whites.

Labor unions in many sectors of the economy have become the institutional expression of the white workers' expectations, based upon the deprivation of the black worker. With the emergence of a new judicial perception of employment discrimination and new legal remedies in the 1970's, organized labor finds itself in increasing conflict with the law. Since Title VII became operative, labor unions have acted to resist compliance in many ways. Among these are: refusing conciliation agreements with the Equal Employment Opportunity Commission, interposing interminable procedural delays in court suits, refusing to comply with Title VII requirements for disclosure of information to the EEOC, and by violating court orders.

More than thirty years after President Franklin D. Roosevelt issued the first fair employment practice Executive Order and eight years after the enactment of the Civil Rights Act of 1964, examination of the extensive body of decisional law reveals that the racial caste system continues to operate in the American economy and that the black worker is confronted by two opponents, corporate enterprise and organized labor, which in the main, each for their own reasons, are still seeking to perpetuate the racist past. When Ashenfelter tells us that there is less discrimination among industrial unions than in craft unions or in the nonunion sector, we must remember that in all three areas discrimination is still a serious problem.

Ronald Oaxaca

SEX DISCRIMINATION IN WAGES[1]

INTRODUCTION

Culture, tradition, and overt discrimination tend to make restrictive the terms by which women may participate in the labor force. These influences combine to generate an unfavorable occupational distribution among female workers vis-à-vis male workers and to create pay differences between males and females within the same occupation. The result is a chronic earnings gap between male and female full-time, year-round workers. Unfortunately, explanations at this level of generality are mainly descriptive. It is the purpose of this paper to estimate the average extent of discrimination against female workers and to provide a quantitative assessment of the causes of male-female wage differentials.

The theoretical framework is discussed in Part 1. The concept of a discrimination coefficient is introduced, and a wage model is developed along the lines of the post-schooling investment model of human capital theory. The empirical results are presented and evaluated in Part 2. Part 3 is a summary and conclusion.

[1] This paper has benefited from useful comments by Orley Ashenfelter, Daniel Hamermesh, and Albert Rees. Financial assistance for this study was provided by the U.S. Department of Labor, Manpower Administration, under the provisions of Title 1 of the Manpower Development and Training Act, Public Law 87-415, as amended. Naturally, the responsibility for any errors lies with the author.

124

1. THEORETICAL FRAMEWORK

A Measure of Discrimination

Discrimination against females can be said to exist whenever the relative wage of males exceeds the relative wage that would have prevailed if males and females were paid according to the same criteria. We can formalize this notion by introducing the concept of a discrimination coefficient (D) as a proposed measure of discrimination: the discrimination coefficient is defined as the proportionate difference between the currently observed male-female wage ratio and the wage ratio that would prevail in the absence of discrimination. The discrimination coefficient can be approximated by the difference between the natural logarithm of the observed male-female wage ratio and the natural logarithm of the wage ratio in the absence of discrimination.[2]

Gary Becker first introduced the concept of a discrimination coefficient.[3] Becker's market discrimination coefficient is defined as the gross wage differential between two types of perfectly substitutable labor. He briefly discusses a generalized market discrimination coefficient that applies to two factors that are not necessarily perfect substitutes for each other. This generalized discrimination coefficient is defined as the simple difference between the observed relative wage of one of the factors and the relative wage that would prevail in the absence of discrimination. Our own measure

[2] Let $D = \dfrac{W_m/W_f - (W_m/W_f)^0}{(W_m/W_f)^0}$; where

W_m/W_f = the observed male-female wage ratio; and
$(W_m/W_f)^0$ = the male-female wage ratios in the absence of discrimination.

An equivalent expression in terms of natural logarithms is given by

$$\ln(D+1) = \ln(W_m/W_f) - \ln(W_m/W_f)^0.$$

[3] Gary S. Becker, *The Economics of Discrimination* (Chicago: University of Chicago Press, 1957), p. 9.

125

of discrimination is simply Becker's generalized measure divided by the wage ratio in the absence of discrimination. Our definition of the discrimination coefficient treats perfect substitutes as a special case.

Since we only observe the current male-female wage ratio but do not observe the wage ratio in the absence of discrimination, the estimation of the discrimination coefficient is equivalent to estimating the male-female wage ratio that would prevail in a nondiscriminating labor market. However, we can estimate this ratio on the basis of either of two assumptions: If there were no discrimination, (1) the wage structure currently faced by females would also apply to males; or (2) the wage structure currently faced by males would also apply to females. Assumption one (two) says that females (males) would on average receive in the absence of discrimination the same wages as they presently receive, but that discrimination takes the form of males (females) receiving more (less) than a nondiscriminating labor market would award them. Actually, the wage structure in the absence of discrimination would probably lie somewhere between the structures implied by assumptions one and two.

Wage Model

The socio-economic characteristics of a large sample of workers determine what we are to regard as the wage structure. Ordinary least squares estimation of a wage equation for any given group of workers provides an estimate of the wage structure applicable to that group. This approach involves relating an individual's wage rate to his level of schooling, experience, and certain other personal attributes. The dependent variable in our equations is the natural logarithm of the wage rate, so that the coefficient estimates are interpreted as the percentage effects of changes in the explanatory variables on the wage rate. The specification of our wage equation is motivated by the post-schooling investment model of human capital formation.[4] Accordingly, the coefficients corresponding to the experience variable can be related to certain on-the-job training (O.J.T.) parameters: the average rate of return to O.J.T., the fraction of time invested in O.J.T. during the first period of work following the completion of formal schooling, and the length of the investment horizon.[5]

Data on the actual number of years of work experience for a large sample of workers are generally unavailable. Accordingly, we use potential experience as a proxy for actual experience. Potential experience is defined as age minus years of formal schooling minus six years. The implications of using the number of years since the completion of formal schooling as a substitute for the number of years of actual work experience can easily be explained with the aid of simple diagrams. Figure 1 shows two possible relationships between actual work experience and potential work experience. If there were no substantial interruptions in work experience, the number of years of work experience would equal the number of years of potential experience until retirement. The 45-degree line through the origin describes this relationship. Now suppose that an individual temporarily stops working X_1 years after the completion of formal schooling and resumes working $X_2 - X_1$ years later. Figure 2 shows what the potential experience-wage profile would look like under these circumstances. It is clear that the number of years of potential experience at which the hourly wage peaks will exceed the number of years in terms of actual work experience by $X_2 - X_1$. One can generalize the analysis by allowing for more than one period of absence

[4] Jacob Mincer, "The Distribution of Labor Incomes: A Survey with Special Reference to the Human Capital Approach," *Journal of Economic Literature*, 8, No. 1 (March 1970), 6-18.

[5] For a more thorough account of the derivation of these O.J.T. parameters from the coefficients on the experience variable see Ronald L. Oaxaca, "Male-Female Wage Differentials in Urban Labor Markets," unpublished Doctoral Dissertation, Princeton University, Economics Department, 1971.

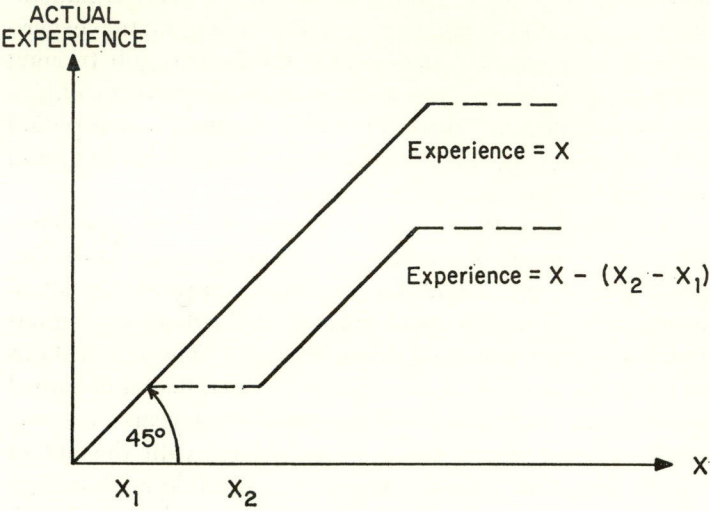

FIGURE 1. Actual and potential experience.

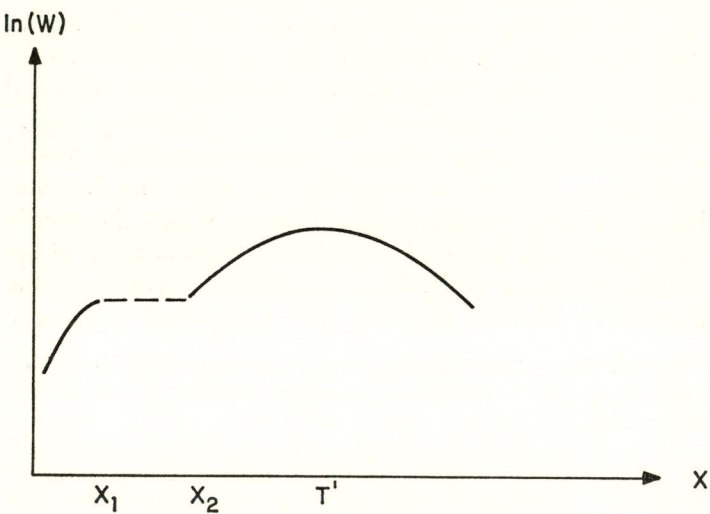

FIGURE 2. Wage-potential experience profile.

128

from work and by not assuming that a person resumes work where he left off without a reduction in the value of accumulated experience via depreciation of human capital. However, these modifications do not change the conclusion in any essential way.

Although the values of X_1 and X_2 vary across individuals, it is clear that ordinary least squares estimation of the potential experience-wage profile will tend to overstate the average number of years of experience at which the hourly wage peaks and to yield a profile that is flatter than the actual experience profile. The extent of overstatement can be expected to vary by race and sex.

These considerations are crucial to any evaluation of the differences between the estimated experience-wage profiles of male and female workers. Potential experience is probably a reasonable approximation of actual years of work experience for males because of their strong attachment to the labor force. On the other hand, at any given time many female workers have been out of the labor force for some period in the past because of their household and childbearing activities. We can expect the estimated experience-wage profile to overstate the length of the investment period for women workers, e.g., in Figure 2, T' exceeds actual T by $X_2 - X_1$ years.

As a rough attempt to handle this problem, let us assume that the number of years of work experience lost is some function of the number of children born to the female. The variable for the number of children ever born to a female enters our wage equation in a linear form, and its coefficient is expected to have a negative sign. A proxy for the relationship between the number of children ever born to a female and the number of years of potential work experience lost can be derived by (1) setting the potential experience profile equal to the children term, (2) solving the resulting quadratic for the appropriate root, and (3) multiplying through by minus one and expressing the result as a function of the number of children. This procedure translates

129

the cost of children (in terms of their effect on the hourly wage) into an equivalent number of years of potential experience.

To the extent that blacks lose more work experience due to more frequent and longer spells of unemployment than whites, the estimated experience-wage profiles for blacks will tend to overstate the length of their investment periods.

The average effect of health limitations on the hourly wage is estimated by introducing a dummy variable that takes the value 1 if the individual reports any health impairment that limits the kind and/or amount of work he can perform, and 0 otherwise.

Migration is a form of investment in human capital, and it should be expected to have some effect on the wage rate. Since this study is not concerned with migration per se, the migration variable acts as a control variable. The specification used involves a two-part migration variable: a dummy regressor and the quadratic form of a continuous variable. The continuous variable is defined as the number of years since the person last migrated. An individual is considered to be a migrant if he moved to his current residence from more than fifty miles away since his seventeenth birthday. The dummy regressor takes the value 1 if the person is a migrant, and 0 otherwise. Both recent migrants and non-migrants will show zero years since they last migrated; however, we might expect that, other things being equal, the recent migrant will receive a lower hourly wage than the nonmigrant. Generally, the recent migrant needs some time in which to become familiar with the best job opportunities open to him in his new location. The dummy regressor differentiates between recent migrants and nonmigrants, and its coefficient is therefore expected to have a negative sign.

We control for the effects of part-time employment by specifying a dummy variable that takes the value 1 if the individual reports that he normally works part-time, and 0 otherwise. For our purposes part-time employment refers to a work week of less than thirty-five hours.

A marital status control variable that is included in the wage equation consists of separate dummy regressors for spouse present, spouse absent, widowed, and divorced. The reference group is people who have never married.

Our wage equations include industry and occupation variables that are defined by dummy regressors for each two-digit Census industry and occupation. Workers in the retail trade are the industry reference group, and sales workers are the occupation reference group.

Differences between urban areas in terms of cost of living, availability of job opportunities, and nonpecuniary factors are related to differences in the sizes of their populations. Since such differences can be important in explaining the variation in wages, the size of urban area is used as a proxy variable in the wage regressions. Dummy regressors are defined for 1) SMSA's (Standard Metropolitan Statistical Areas) less than 250,000; 2) SMSA's of 250,000 or greater but less than 500,000; 3) SMSA's of 500,000 or greater but less than 750,000; and 4) SMSA's of 750,000 or greater. The reference group is urban areas outside SMSA's.

The effects of geographic region are controlled for by separate dummy regressors for three of the four Census regions: North East, North Central, and West. The South serves as the reference region.

Workers who belong to unions generally earn higher hourly wages than they would receive if they were not union members. Since the separate effects of industry, occupation, city size, and region have been controlled for, some confidence can be placed in the estimated coefficient on the unionism dummy regressor as an estimate of the unionism effect.

One difficulty with the present formulation of the wage equation is that it controls for many of the sources of dis-

131

crimination against women. By controlling for major occupation, we eliminate much of the effects of occupational barriers as sources of discrimination. As a result, we are likely to underestimate seriously the effects of discrimination.[6] Consequently, we estimate another set of equations that do not control for occupation, industry, and union membership. We shall refer to this set of regressions as the personal characteristics wage regressions, and to the original set as the full-scale wage regressions.

2. ESTIMATION OF THE MODEL

Data Source

The 1967 Survey of Economic Opportunity is the primary source of data for this study. The survey was conducted for the Office of Economic Opportunity by the Bureau of the Census in February 1967. The data pertain to approximately 60,000 individuals in 30,000 households across the United States. Detailed information is provided on an individual's place of residence, industry of employment, occupation, and personal characteristics. The particular subsample used for this study consists of the intersection of the following sets: those individuals who show an hourly wage for the week preceding the survey; adults sixteen years or older; those who live in urban areas; and those who report their race as either *White* or *Negro*.

Empirical Results

The regression coefficients corresponding to the full-scale wage equations are presented in Table 1, and the coeffi-

[6] See, for example, Henry Sanborn, "Pay Differences Between Men and Women," *Industrial and Labor Relations Review*, 17 (July 1964), 534-550. Sanborn standardized the female-male income ratio for differences in occupational distribution at the three digit level. This method implicitly defined discrimination to be unequal pay for equal work. Not surprisingly, Sanborn found that discrimination defined in this way accounted for very little of the overall income difference between males and females.

132

TABLE 1

Full-Scale Wage Regressions

(*t* Values in parentheses)

Dependent Variable log (hourly wage)	White Males	White Females	Black Males	Black Females
Independent Variables:				
Constant	.0365	—.1024	.0953	—.3851
	(.77)	(—1.34)	(1.71)	(—6.35)
Experience				
Experience	.0176	.0138	.0117	.0067
	(13.89)	(8.19)	(7.73)	(4.38)
Experience **2	—.000288	—.000248	—.000204	—.000122
	(—12.22)	(—7.31)	(—7.59)	(—4.33)
Education				
Education	.0082	—.0118	—.0308	—.0175
	(1.27)	(—.98)	(—4.60)	(—1.98)
Education**2	.00169	.00194	.00300	.00245
	(5.92)	(3.53)	(8.23)	(5.26)
Class of worker				
Union	.1113	.1500	.2129	.0719
	(9.39)	(6.70)	(14.15)	(3.11)
Nonunion Private wage and salary	—	—	—	—
Government	.0646	.1445	.1328	.1263
	(3.15)	(5.89)	(5.44)	(5.19)
Selfemployed	—.1290	.1137	—.0128	—.3437
	(3.51)	(1.22)	(—.15)	(—2.67)
Industry				
Agriculture	.1285	.2847	—.0067	—.0190
	(1.81)	(1.09)	(—.08)	(—.21)
Mining	.3604	.4112	.0697	—
	(6.83)	(2.02)	(.40)	
Construction	.2997	.2444	.2729	.0395
	(13.72)	(3.80)	(10.54)	(.22)

133

TABLE 1 (*continued*)

Dependent Variable log (hourly wage)	White Males	White Females	Black Males	Black Females
Manufacturing—durable	.2398	.2562	.2101	.2590
	(13.76)	(8.39)	(9.15)	(6.46)
Manufacturing—non durable	.2086	.1968	.1679	.2305
	(11.03)	(6.60)	(6.85)	(6.46)
Transportation	.2332	.3154	.2182	.5463
	(9.81)	(5.54)	(7.39)	(5.73)
Communications	.2370	.2290	.1555	.2657
	(5.62)	(4.56)	(1.78)	(3.71)
Utilities	.2414	.2451	.1433	.7026
	(7.32)	(2.83)	(3.45)	(2.76)
Wholesale Trade	.2039	.1979	.1204	.3065
	(8.45)	(4.74)	(3.76)	(4.34)
Retail Trade	—	—	—	—
Finance	.2224	.1761	.0184	.1593
	(8.25)	(5.65)	(.47)	(3.22)
Business and repair services	.1385	.1525	.0766	.1326
	(4.44)	(3.24)	(2.10)	(2.31)
Personal services	—.0618	—.0183	—.1055	.0118
	(—1.71)	(—.50)	(—3.22)	(.40)
Recreation	.0488	.1527	.0020	.1019
	(.97)	(1.97)	(.04)	(1.29)
Professional services	—.0629	.0528	.0633	.1181
	(—2.53)	(2.01)	(2.13)	(4.45)

134

TABLE 1 *(continued)*

Dependent Variable
log (hourly wage)

	White Males	White Females	Black Males	Black Females
Public administration	.1970	.2165	.2374	.2170
	(6.58)	(4.86)	(6.75)	(5.61)
Occupation Professional workers	.1563	.3736	.2144	.4631
	(6.62)	(10.25)	(4.62)	(10.80)
Managers	.1822	.2759	.0810	.2792
	(8.27)	(6.85)	(1.49)	(3.53)
Clerical workers	—.0639	.1665	.0208	.1509
	(—2.68)	(6.03)	(.54)	(4.50)
Sales workers	—	—	—	—
Craftsmen	.0275	.0932	.0733	.1297
	(1.28)	(1.31)	(1.99)	(1.97)
Operatives	—.1064	.0128	—.0271	.0236
	(—4.92)	(.37)	(—.77)	(.62)
Private household workers	—.1900	—.3060	—.0458	—.1432
	(—1.03)	(—5.46)	(—.28)	(—3.58)
Service workers	—.1358	—.0219	—.0998	—.0164
	(—5.19)	(—.72)	(—2.84)	(—.53)
Farm laborers	—.4750	.1579	—.1421	—
	(—5.38)	(.43)	(—1.36)	—
Laborers	—.1540	—.0166	—.0537	.0317
	(—5.59)	(—.15)	(—1.77)	(.37)
Health Problems	—.1001	—.0710	—.0811	—.0270
	(—6.08)	(—2.70)	(—3.79)	(—1.31)

135

TABLE 1 (continued)

Dependent Variable log (hourly wage)	White Males	White Females	Black Males	Black Females
Part-Time	—.1874	—.0445	—.1117	.0034
	(—9.14)	(—2.64)	(—4.80)	(.21)
Migration				
Migration	—.0356	—.1073	.0052	—.0361
	(—2.48)	(—5.03)	(.44)	(—1.94)
YRSM	.0072	.0087	—	.0025
	(4.22)	(3.33)	—	(2.73)
YRSM**2	—.000140	—.000147	—	—
	(—3.08)	(—2.14)	—	—
Marital Status				
Spouse Present	.1841	.0883	.1211	.0995
	(11.88)	(4.51)	(6.43)	(5.13)
Spouse Absent	.1124	.0852	.0446	.1050
	(1.72)	(1.39)	(.79)	(2.38)
Widowed	.1030	.0687	.0920	.0980
	(2.37)	(2.21)	(2.13)	(3.47)
Divorced	.0793	.0933	.0396	.0607
	(2.74)	(3.38)	(1.53)	(2.72)
Never Married	—	—	—	—
Children	—	—.0198	—	—.0007
	—	(—4.51)	—	(—.24)
Size of Urban Area				
Urban, Non SMSA	—	—	—	—
SMSA 250	.0332	.0920	.0523	.1458
	(1.98)	(3.86)	(1.54)	(4.19)
SMSA 500	.0727	.0956	.1098	.1833
	(3.89)	(3.65)	(2.83)	(4.61)
SMSA 750	.1411	.1524	.1349	.1316
	(7.30)	(5.46)	(3.55)	(4.46)

TABLE 1 (*continued*)

Dependent Variable log (hourly wage)	White Males	White Females	Black Males	Black Females
SMSA 750+	.1745	.2186	.2079	.3643
	(12.57)	(11.21)	(6.46)	(10.92)
Region				
North East	.0738	.0882	.1366	.1724
	(5.63)	(4.69)	(7.86)	(9.24)
North Central	.0749	.0646	.1479	.1376
	(5.85)	(3.52)	(9.37)	(8.00)
South	—	—	—	—
West	.1200	.1389	.2452	.2612
	(8.51)	(6.83)	(12.48)	(12.07)
Years of experience at which the hourly wage peaks	30.6	27.8	28.7	27.5
R^2	.43	.33	.46	.56
S.E.E	.4034	.4510	.3493	.3560
NOBS	8123	4962	3897	3502

cients corresponding to the personal characteristics wage equations are presented in Table 2. Coefficients were not estimated in the following cases: 1) the particular characteristic served as the base group; 2) there were no observations in a particular cell; 3) the same observations were found in another cell (perfect multicollinearity); or 4) the regression was left out on the basis of poor results from earlier regressions.

Space limitations do not permit a complete discussion of the regression results; therefore we shall restrict our attention to only a few selected aspects of the regressions.[7]

---

[7] For a more detailed analysis of the regression results, see my dissertation, *op. cit.*

TABLE 2

Personal Characteristics Wage Regressions

(*t* Values in parentheses)

Dependent Variable: log (hourly wage)				
	White Males	White Females	Black Males	Black Females
Independent Variables:				
Constant	—.0681	.0894	.1472	—.2325
	(—2.03)	(.94)	(2.44)	(—3.75)
Experience				
Experience	.0222	.0182	.0195	.0066
	(16.51)	(10.20)	(12.03)	(4.02)
Experience **2	—.000354	—.000349	—.000340	—.000133
	(—14.19)	(—9.69)	(—11.69)	(—4.26)
Education				
Education	.0342	—.0394	—.0434	—.0660
	(5.24)	(—3.30)	(—6.16)	(—7.12)
Education **2	.00097	.00450	.00417	.00685
	(3.51)	(8.63)	(11.46)	(15.35)
Health				
Problems	—.1325	—.1097	—.1275	—.0638
	(—7.57)	(—3.89)	(—5.41)	(—2.75)
Part-Time	—.3154	—.1560	—.1908	—.1139
	(—14.84)	(—9.09)	(—7.57)	(—6.73)
Migration				
Migration	—.0316	—.1262	.0125	—.0726
	(—2.08)	(—5.54)	(.96)	(—3.48)
YRSM	.0073	.0107	—	.0034
	(3.98)	(3.81)		(3.24)
YRSM**2	—.000140	—.000169	—	—
	(—2.91)	(—2.29)		

TABLE 2 (*continued*)

Dependent Variable log (hourly wage)				
	White Males	*White Females*	*Black Males*	*Black Females*
Marital Status				
Spouse				
present	.2514	.1246	.1584	.0986
	(15.44)	(5.96)	(7.66)	(4.53)
Spouse				
absent	.1189	.0706	.0975	.0964
	(1.71)	(1.07)	(1.56)	(1.94)
Widowed	.1389	.0804	.1648	.0754
	(3.00)	(2.41)	(3.46)	(2.38)
Divorced	.1027	.1064	.0511	.0618
	(3.34)	(3.61)	(1.78)	(2.46)
Never				
married	—	—	—	—
Children	—	—.0295	—	—.0025
		(—6.31)		(—.80)
Size of Urban Area				
Urban, Non				
SMSA	—	—	—	—
SMSA 250	.0412	.1080	.0667	.1415
	(2.30)	(4.23)	(1.78)	(3.60)
SMSA 500	.0845	.1154	.1103	.1879
	(4.26)	(4.11)	(2.57)	(4.20)
SMSA 750	.1739	.1721	.1821	.1769
	(8.47)	(5.77)	(4.34)	(3.86)
SMSA 750+	.1972	.2543	.2452	.3888
	(13.45)	(12.27)	(6.95)	(10.39)
Region				
North East	.0655	.1129	.1704	.2268
	(4.73)	(5.69)	(8.97)	(11.07)
North				
Central	.0790	.0685	.2255	.1996
	(5.91)	(3.52)	(13.56)	(10.57)

TABLE 2 (*continued*)

Dependent Variable log (hourly wage)				
	White Males	White Females	Black Males	Black Females
South	—	—	—	—
West	.1111	.1174	.2889	.3027
	(7.49)	(5.43)	(13.44)	(12.56)
Years of experience at which the hourly wage peaks	31.4	26.1	28.8	24.8
R^2	.34	.22	.33	.43
S.E.E.	.4308	.4851	.3879	.4026
NOBS	8123	4962	3897	3502

The Survey of Economic Opportunity data report membership in a union only for private wage and salary workers; therefore, we can only examine the effect of unionism on the wages of this group of workers. Accordingly, we define dummy regressors for government employees, union membership of private wage and salary workers, and self-employed.[8] Table 1 reveals that all four groups enjoy a union/nonunion wage advantage, but black females benefit the least with an estimated union/nonunion wage differential of only 7 percent. The modest unionism effect for black females may suggest that black female unionists are concentrated in weak unions.

An important question concerns the effect of unionism on the male-female wage ratio. The answer to this question requires an examination of differences in the proportions of

[8] The method by which the subsample was selected effectively eliminated most of the self-employed because their incomes were not generally recorded in the form of wages or salary; nevertheless there were some individuals who reported a wage or salary, yet considered themselves self-employed.

workers unionized as well as differences in the union/non-union wage differential between males and females. The data show that 28 percent of the white males in the sample are members of unions as opposed to only 12 percent of white females, and 32 percent of the black males are union members as opposed to only 11 percent of black females. For a given group of workers, the effect of unionism on the average hourly wage relative to the nonunion wage is computed by multiplying the union/nonunion wage differential (the estimated coefficient on the unionism dummy regressor) by the extent of unionism for that group. The difference between this unionism effect for males and females can be interpreted as a measure of the effect of unionism on the average male-female wage ratio.[9] The findings of this study suggest that in the absence of unionism the male-female wage ratio would be 1.3 percent lower for whites and 6 percent lower for blacks. Thus the presence of unions raises the wages of males relative to females.

The results in Tables 1 and 2 suggest that the estimated experience-wage profiles are flatter and peak earlier for females. If the rate of return to on-the-job training were the same for males and females, then the estimated coefficients of the experience variable would imply that males invest more in O.J.T. initially and for a longer period than females. On the other hand, if we believe that males and females have the same initial investment in O.J.T., then the estimated parameters of the experience variable imply that the rate of return for females relative to that of males is less than the length of the females' investment horizon relative to the males'. Unfortunately, our approach does not allow us to uniquely estimate the key O.J.T. parameters.

It is apparent from Tables 1 and 2 that children have a

---

[9] We are implicitly assuming that the effects of unionism on the non-union wage are the same for males and females. For a comprehensive treatment of this topic in the context of black-white wage differentials see Orley Ashenfelter, "Racial Discrimination and Trade Unionism," *Journal of Political Economy*, 80 (May/June 1972), 435-464.

significant negative effect on the hourly wages of white females but a negligible effect in the case of black females. These results would seem to imply that black females do not stay out of work as long for each child born as do white females. Our results are consistent with those empirical studies of labor supply which tend to find that the presence of children, especially preschool-age children, inhibits the labor force participation of white females significantly more than for black females.[10] If black females tended to remain out of the labor force for as long as white females each time a child is born, the effects of children on wages through their effect on experience would still be less for black females to the extent that experience is not very important in the types of jobs they typically hold. Estimates of an equivalent number of years of experience lost per child are presented in Table 3 for white females only. These estimates were calculated according to the method described in the theoretical section of this paper.

TABLE 3

Estimates of Work Experience Lost Due to Childbearing

Number of Children	Equivalent Number of Years of Experience	
	Full-Scale Wage Regression	Personal Characteristics Wage Regression
1	1.4	1.6
2	2.7	3.1
3	4.0	4.5
4	5.2	5.9

[10] William G. Bowen and T. A. Finegan, *The Economics of Labor Force Participation* (Princeton, N.J.: Princeton University Press, 1969), pp. 96-105; and Glen G. Cain, *Married Women in the Labor Force: An Economic Analysis* (Chicago: The University of Chicago Press, 1966), pp. 72-81.

The Effects of Discrimination

The average hourly wages computed from our sample are as follows: $2.95 for white males, $1.92 for white females, $2.16 for black males and $1.45 for black females.[11] The male-female gross wage differential (G) implied by these wage figures is 54 percent for whites and 49 percent for blacks.[12]

When the gross wage differential is expressed in terms of natural logarithms, the formulation of the discrimination coefficient implies that the differential can be decomposed into the effects of discrimination and the effects of differences in personal characteristics. Our method for estimating the effects of discrimination involves an index number problem. A range of possible values of the discrimination coefficient is obtained from the separate estimates yielded by the use of the female and male wage structures.

The estimated percentage effects of discrimination and differences in personal characteristics on the gross wage differential are presented in Table 4. These percentage figures are obtained by expressing the calculated effects of discrimination and differences in personal characteristics as percentages of the overall male-female wage differential (in terms of natural logarithms).

The percentage effects corresponding to the regressors that constitute a variable are added together to yield the total percentage effect of the variable. In the case of whites, the results show that discrimination accounts for approximately 78 percent of the gross wage differential in terms of natural logarithms. Much of the impact on the gross wage differential from differences in personal characteristics can

[11] These average wage figures are computed as geometric means, i.e.,

$$W = \exp \sum_{i=1}^{N} (\ln(W_i))/N.$$

[12] $G = \dfrac{\overline{W}_m - \overline{W}_f}{\overline{W}}$

TABLE 4

The Effects of Discrimination and Personal Characteristics on the Male-Female Wage Differential[a]
(Natural Logarithms)

| | Whites | | | |
| | Female Regression Weights | | Male Regression Weights | |
	$\hat{b}_{f1}(\bar{Z}_{mj} - \bar{Z}_{f1})$	Percentage Effects	$\hat{b}_{mj}(\bar{Z}_{mj} - \bar{Z}_{f1})$	Percentage Effects
Gross Differential:	$\ln (G + 1) = .4307$		$\ln (G + 1) = .4307$	
Personal Characteristics:				
Experience	.0072	1.7	.0094	2.1
Education	.0122	2.8	.0008	0.2
Health Problems	−.0018	−0.4	−.0022	−0.5
Part-Time	.0227	5.3	.0459	10.7
Migration	−.0033	−0.8	.0002	0.0
Marital Status	.0143	3.3	.0380	8.8
Children	.0460	10.7	.0000	0.0
Size of Urban Area	.0017	0.4	.0012	0.3
Region	−.0003	−0.1	.0001	0.0
$-\Sigma_j \hat{b}_{f1}(\bar{Z}_{mj} - \bar{Z}_{f1}) = -.0987$		77.1		
$-\Sigma_j \hat{b}_{mj}(\bar{Z}_{mj} - \bar{Z}_{f1}) = -.0934$				78.3
Discrimination:				
	$\ln (D + 1) = .3320$		$\ln (D + 1) = .3373$	

TABLE 4 (continued)

Blacks

	Female Regression Weights		Male Regression Weights	
	$\hat{b}_{fj}\,(\bar{Z}_{mj}-\bar{Z}_{fj})$	Percentage Effects	$\hat{b}_{mj}\,(\bar{Z}_{mj}-\bar{Z}_{fj})$	Percentage Effects
Gross Differential:				
	$\ln\,(G+1)=.3989$		$\ln\,(G+1)=.3989$	
Personal Characteristics:				
Experience	—.0007	—0.2	.0028	0.7
Education	—.0351	—8.8	—.0190	—4.8
Health Problems	.0015	0.4	.0030	0.8
Part-Time	.0187	4.7	.0314	7.9
Migration	—.0024	—0.6	.0004	0.1
Marital Status	.0086	2.2	.0167	4.2
Children	.0052	1.3	.0000	0.0
Size of Urban Area	.0033	0.8	.0029	0.7
Region	.0058	1.5	.0069	1.7
	$-\Sigma_j\,\hat{b}_{fj}\,(\bar{Z}_{mj}-\bar{Z}_{fj})=-.0049$		$-\Sigma_j\,\hat{b}_{mj}\,(\bar{Z}_{mj}-\bar{Z}_{fj})=-.0451$	
Discrimination:				
	$\ln\,(D+1)=.3940$	98.8	$\ln\,(D+1)=.3538$	88.7

[a] The estimated coefficient $\hat{b}_{fj}$ and $\hat{b}_{mj}$ refer to the jth variable from the female and male regressions. The term '$\bar{Z}_{mj}-\bar{Z}_{fj}$' is the difference in the mean values of the jth regressor for males and females. Thus $\Sigma_j\hat{b}_{fj}(\bar{Z}_{mj}-\bar{Z}_{fj})$ is the total effect of the differences in personal characteristics.

be attributed to the effects of children, marital status, and part-time employment. In the case of blacks, the results suggest that discrimination accounts for approximately 94 percent of the gross wage differential in terms of natural logarithms. Since the index number phenomenon is more apparent for blacks, the effect of discrimination is calculated as a simple average of the two independent estimates. Much of the impact on the gross differential from differences in personal characteristics can be attributed to the effects of schooling, marital status, and part-time employment. While marital status and part-time employment tend to widen the gross wage differential for blacks, the effect of schooling is to narrow the differential, because black female workers have significantly more schooling than black male workers.

The calculated values of the discrimination coefficient (D) are presented in Table 5. If the discrimination coeffi-

TABLE 5

Estimates of the Discrimination Coefficient[a]

	Whites		Blacks	
Assumptions:				
Female Wage Structure	.39	(.32)	.48	(.27)
Male Wage Structure	.40	(.25)	.42	(.22)

[a] The figures in parentheses were estimated on the basis of the full scale wage regressions.

cient is taken as the midpoint of the range of values given in Table 5, then D equals .40 for whites and .45 for blacks. Given that the gross differential G equals .54 and .49 for whites and blacks, respectively, the discrimination coefficient accounts for approximately 74 percent of the male-female wage differential for whites and 92 percent for

146

blacks.[13] The difference between the gross wage differential and the discrimination coefficient yields an estimate of the wage differential that would prevail in the absence of discrimination: this differential is approximately .14 for whites and .04 for blacks.

As we have noted above, the full-scale wage regressions are expected to yield rather conservative estimates of the effects of discrimination. Values of D calculated under these circumstances are presented in parentheses in Table 5. If we calculate D as the midpoint of the range of possible values given in Table 5, then the discrimination coefficient is approximately .29 for whites and .25 for blacks. These figures imply that discrimination accounts for only 53 percent of the wage differential for whites and 52 percent for blacks.

3. CONCLUDING REMARKS

The very substantial influence of discrimination on the observed male-female wage differential is the single most important finding of this study. When the discrimination coefficient is taken to be the midpoint of the range of values presented in Table 5, the coefficient equals .40 and .45 for whites and blacks, respectively. If one considers that the gross wage differential is .54 for whites and .49 for blacks, discrimination accounts for a significant portion of the observed wage differentials. These estimates imply that discrimination can account for approximately 74 percent of the gross wage differential for whites and 92 percent for blacks. In the absence of sex discrimination as we have defined it, the average female wage as a percentage of the average male wage would be 88 percent for white females and 96

[13] These percentages differ slightly from those calculated in terms of natural logarithms because of differences between the ratios

$$\frac{\ln (D + 1)}{\ln (G + 1)} \text{ and } \frac{D}{G}.$$

147

percent for black females (the current percentages are 65 and 67 percent for whites and blacks, respectively). These figures imply a residual wage differential of approximately 14 percent for whites and 4 percent for blacks. Much of the remaining differential can be attributed to the effects of marital status, childbearing and part-time employment. Our results suggest that virtually all of the gross wage differential between black males and black females is the product of sex discrimination. Also, the combined effects of race and sex discrimination relegate black females to jobs at the very bottom of the occupational ladder.

Government employees of all four race-sex groups benefit relative to their counterparts who are nonunion private wage and salary workers; however white male government workers benefit the least. This finding is consistent with the notion that government engages less in discriminatory employment practices where blacks and females are concerned.

The empirical results reveal some combination of differences in the rate of return to on-the-job training and the extent of investment in on-the-job training for males and females. The hourly wage peaks later for males in terms of measured experience than for females. This result is consistent with the hypothesis that males tend to have a longer investment horizon than females. If the rate of return to O.J.T. were the same for males and females, the estimated parameters of the experience profile would imply that males invest more initially and for a longer period than females. On the other hand, if the initial fraction of time or time equivalent invested in O.J.T. were the same for males and females, then one could only infer that the relative rate of return for females is less than the relative length of their investment horizon.

The effect of the children variable on the hourly wage of white females seems to reflect the loss of actual work experience due to childbearing. Black females, however, do not appear to lose a significant amount of work experience on this account. Perhaps the prevalence of the extended family arrangement in black communities provides a ready source of child care for working mothers.

The policy implications to be discussed are derived from the values implicit in this study. That is to say, the resultant policy recommendations rest on the desire to eliminate sex discrimination as we have defined it. Viewed in this way, our study confirms the necessity of antidiscrimination laws; however, it also indicates that mere passage of such legislation is insufficient to completely eradicate sex discrimination within any reasonable time span.

The Federal Equal Pay Act of 1963 is certainly a welcome ally in the fight against discrimination, but its usefulness is limited to reducing only one form of discrimination. Equal pay legislation is not likely to completely eliminate wage differences between men and women in narrowly defined occupations, much less to have any large-scale effect on the overall male-female wage ratio. As long as some form of market segregation is possible, wage differentials can continue to exist because males and females must receive equal pay for equal work only if they are at the same place of employment.

Title VII of the Civil Rights Act of 1964 is supposed to put an end to sex discriminatory hiring practices; however, available statistics show that women are far more likely to complain to the authorities if they are paid less than men performing the same tasks at the same place of work than if they are not hired for a particular job in the first place.[14]

It is obvious from this study that the removal of all occupational barriers to women would benefit those who take advantage of the new opportunities; nevertheless, the occupational distribution among women would have to change considerably before any discernible effect on their relative wages is noted. There is at least one reason why the removal of all occupational barriers may not have much ini-

[14] See the annual reports from 1967 to 1970 of the U.S. Equal Employment Opportunity Commission (Washington, D.C.: Government Printing Office).

149

tial effect: social conditioning (considered to be insidious by some feminists) starting with childhood experiences is in large part responsible for the seemingly voluntary occupational choices of so many women. Information campaigns on available opportunities as well as the provision for child care centers can overcome the traditional occupational choice pattern of women to some extent.

We see that passive acceptance of the federal guidelines and legislation governing sex discrimination is not sufficient to raise the relative wages of females to the rather conservative estimates given in this study as goals to be attained. Not only should government and private employers actively recruit women for the better-paying jobs that men now hold almost exclusively, but there should also be programs for promoting females already employed. In some cases, female employees will lack the specific training or skills for promotion to the better-paying jobs although they may possess the necessary entry level qualifications in terms of formal educational requirements. Much of this discrepancy can be accommodated by on-the-job training, which is always an important factor in the better-paying jobs.

The results of this study show that unions benefit males relative to females chiefly because of the smaller extent of union membership among female workers. What may appear as union exclusion of female membership is actually occupational exclusion. If females can be encouraged and allowed to enter the higher paying unionized occupations, then the problem of the differential impact of unionism should take care of itself.

If the call for widespread recruiting and training programs on the part of government and private industry seems grandiose, it is because the extent of sex discrimination is widespread and occurs on a large scale. If the policy recommendations of this study seem costly to implement, it is because discrimination is costly to the women involved and its eradication cannot be expected to be cheaply obtained.

Perhaps this study suggests that the reasons behind the magnitude of the current male-female wage differential are more important than the existence of a differential per se. The factors presently accounting for the wage differential indicate an underutilization of the resources and talents of women. This underutilization is the product of social biases and the consequent adaptation to these biases by women. If occupational barriers could be eliminated and women encouraged to exploit their talents to the fullest extent compatible with their own preferences, we could be assured that any observed wage differential is the outcome of voluntary choices affecting occupational attachment and investment in human capital.

Barbara R. Bergmann   COMMENT

In thinking about the gap between white and black incomes many Americans soothe their consciences by choosing to believe that the race gap is due almost entirely to differences in personal characteristics of blacks and whites. Now that the women's movement has focused attention on the gap in pay of men and women, the same kinds of statements are being made about the reasons for the sex gap. In the case of blacks, the finger is pointed at educational deficiency, both in quantity and in quality. That particular excuse (and the word excuse is used advisedly)[1] won't work for women, because the girls sit in the same classrooms as the boys and do about as well. So the finger is pointed at women's lesser attachment to the work force and to the loss in experience which dropping out and dropping in entails. The main contribution of Oaxaca's paper is to demolish the myth that fewer years of experience is an important factor in the lower pay of women. His estimate that experience differences (in terms of years worked) would explain as little as 1.7 percent of the difference in pay and as much as 2.1 percent of it should put to rest that particular canard.

While Oaxaca deserves praise for downgrading the importance of differences in the *quantity* of experience of men and women, the deficiency in the *quality* of women's ex-

[1] The educational achievement of the black community of an SMSA as compared to the whites of that community does not contribute to predicting how well the black community will do in achieving occupational standing as compared to the whites, although, of course, an educated black individual will probably do better than an uneducated one. See Barbara R. Bergmann and Jerolyn R. Lyle, "The Occupational Standing of Negroes in Areas and Industries," *Journal of Human Resources*, Fall, 1971.

perience is, I am convinced, one of the main reasons why women earn less. This quality deficiency in women's experience is, of course, very closely linked to occupational segregation of the sexes.

As Oaxaca properly points out, discrimination and occupational segregation are not unconnected. Discriminatory conduct by employers takes the form of erecting barriers which keep women out of occupations "fitting" for men, and men out of occupations "fitting" for women. As I have argued elsewhere, this kind of employer behavior may result in the overcrowding of occupations considered "fitting" for the inferior group, which in turn leads to low productivity and low wages in those occupations.[2] In the case of women, the steady and considerable increase through time in labor force participation, combined with still strong taboos on expanding the number of occupations thought "fitting" for women have undoubtedly increased the degree of overcrowding in those clerical and service occupations where many women have been employed.

But occupational segregation also has an important effect on the quality of the experience women get. In some jobs the experience the worker gets makes him or her more productive as time passes; in other jobs the experienced are hardly more productive than the novices. Needless to say, jobs of the first kind, in which experience contributes importantly to productivity and enhances earning power, are precisely those jobs which tend to be closed to women. Oaxaca's findings that return to on-the-job training is less for women and that women's earnings peak earlier than men's are really a reflection of the segregation of women into jobs where most of what they learn on the job is learned in the first month. Compare, for example, the learning opportunities of the 22-year-old male management trainee and his 22-year-old female secretary, both of them possibly graduates of the same college. It is no wonder that,

[2] "Effect on White Incomes of Discrimination in Employment," *Journal of Political Economy*, 79 (March/April, 1971), 294-313.

when they get into their forties, he will be earning five times what she is. And the ratio of his earnings to hers will really depend very little on the number of babies she has dropped out to have, or even whether she has dropped out at all.

Oaxaca and a number of other writers tend, when they speak of investment in human capital, to use language implying that the investment is entirely at the option of the employee. For example, Oaxaca says that his estimates "imply that males invest more initially and for a longer period than females." This manner of speaking obscures the fact that people can be excluded from the opportunity to accumulate human capital by discrimination on the part of employers, and that women (and blacks) very frequently are barred from accumulating as much human capital as they would like.

Finally, it should be emphasized that there is a very close connection between the behavior of women with respect to "dropping out" of the labor force and the kinds of jobs which are open to them. There is a kind of vicious-circle phenomenon here. The kinds of jobs to which women are relegated are those which offer little career development and, therefore, little incentive to avoid dropping out for considerable periods. The propensity of these bored women in unchallenging jobs to drop out of the labor force in order to devote themselves to housewifery for long periods is then used as a reason for excluding them from jobs where continuity pays off to employer and employee. We need some studies which provide us with data on the behavior of women in jobs where there are possibilities of advancement. We may hope that the enforcement of anti-discrimination laws and changing attitudes on the part of employers and on the part of women themselves will mean that there will be more such women to study in the future than there are now.

Phyllis A. Wallace EMPLOYMENT
DISCRIMINATION:
SOME POLICY
CONSIDERATIONS

1. INTRODUCTION

After the passage of the Civil Rights Act of 1964 an elaborate Equal Employment Opportunity delivery system was developed by the federal government. Figure 1 outlines in highly schematic form some of the numerous interactions of individuals and organizations which have shaped policy for equal employment opportunity for women and minority workers. Social scientists, especially economists, have only recently turned their attention to the difficult analytical problems of defining employment discrimination and suggesting appropriate remedies.[1] Although the studies by Becker, Thurow, and Arrow are important additions to economic literature, they have not produced analytical models that could be used for policy planning.[2]

This paper attempts to assess the present status of equal employment opportunity and to present some alternative

[1] It is appropriate that Princeton University should sponsor a conference on "Discrimination in Labor Markets" approximately four years after the Industrial Relations Section undertook a project to analyze for the U.S. Equal Employment Opportunity Commission data from the first annual report on minority employment patterns (the EEO-1 employer reporting system).

[2] For further analyses see Gary S. Becker, *The Economics of Discrimination* (Chicago: University of Chicago Press, 1957); Lester C. Thurow, *Poverty and Discrimination* (Washington, D.C.: The Brookings Institution, 1969); and Kenneth Arrow, "The Theory of Discrimination," in this volume.

155

strategies of intervention. The perspective partly reflects my experiences in working three years at the U.S. Equal Employment Opportunity Commission and the presumption that elimination of employment discrimination (differential valuation of labor input of equal productivity) is regarded as a desirable social norm.

FEDERAL EEO DELIVERY SYSTEMS

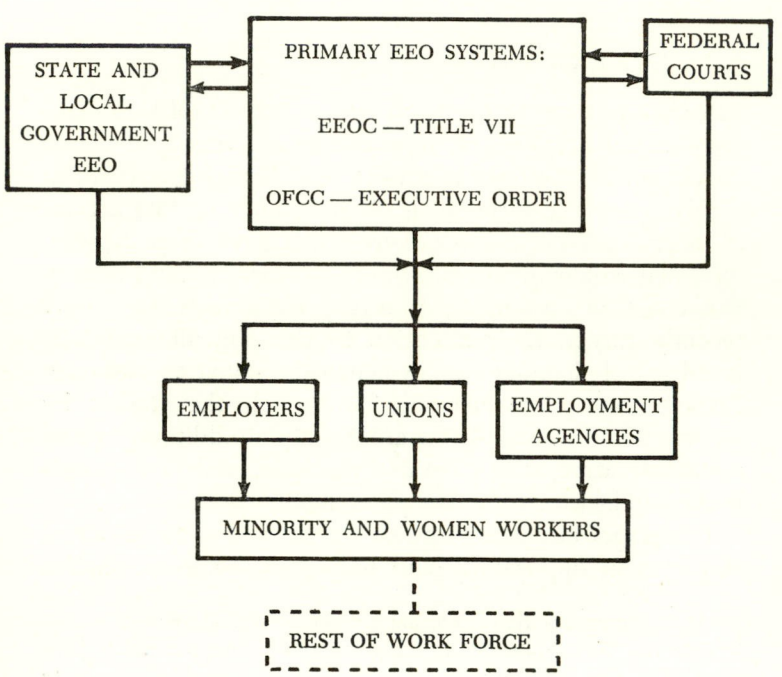

The four primary components of the federal EEO delivery system are discussed in Sections 2, 3, 4, and 5. Progress since 1965 and alternative strategies are examined in the last two sections of this paper.

156

2. THE FEDERAL EQUAL EMPLOYMENT OPPORTUNITY DELIVERY SYSTEM

A variety of laws, executive orders, regulations, and legal decisions prohibit discrimination in employment in the public and private sectors. The proscription is against discrimination based on race, color, sex, religion, or national origin. Title VII of the Civil Rights Act of 1964 prohibits employers, unions, employment agencies (public and private), and joint labor management committees controlling apprenticeship or other training programs from discriminating in hiring and discharging; in compensation, terms, conditions or privileges of employment; in classifying; in assigning or promoting employees; in extending or assigning use of facilities; and in admission to training, retraining, or apprenticeship programs. This act, which became effective on July 2, 1965, is administered by the U.S. Equal Employment Opportunity Commission (EEOC), a small independent agency in the federal executive branch. The Equal Employment Opportunity Act of 1972[3] has amended Title VII by expanding its coverage to include employees of state and local governments and of educational institutions, as well as private employment of more than fifteen persons.

Executive Order No. 11246, as amended by Executive Order No. 11375, prohibits employment discrimination by federal government contractors, subcontractors, and federally assisted construction contractors. Under regulations issued by the Office of Federal Contract Compliance (OFCC) of the Department of Labor, federal contractors with a contract of $50,000 or more and fifty or more employees must develop a written plan of affirmative action to insure equal employment opportunity. Federal contractors are required to establish goals and timetables to achieve this objective.

[3] Public Law 92-261, 92nd Congress, H.R. 1746.

Until passage of the Equal Employment Opportunity Act of 1972, the three million civilian employees of the U.S. Government were provided equal opportunity under Executive Order No. 11246 as amended and Executive Order No. 11478. The U.S. Civil Service Commission was responsible for the implementation of these orders. In 1972 federal employees for the first time have been brought under Title VII of the Civil Rights Act of 1964.

3. EQUAL EMPLOYMENT OPPORTUNITY COMMISSION

An examination of the core system for the delivery of EEO to minority and women workers in the private sector reveals that prior to 1972 the EEOC did not have enforcement powers and had to investigate and attempt conciliation of complaints alleging discrimination. The burden of seeking enforcement through the federal courts rested mainly on the aggrieved person. The Commission referred to the U.S. Attorney General selected cases involving a pattern or practice of discrimination and filed as a friend of the court in private actions. Lacking an enforcement apparatus to deal with the vastly more complex social, economic, and philosophical issues of the late sixties, the Commission had regularly sought to have Title VII amended.

The most significant change introduced by the Equal Employment Opportunity Act of 1972 authorizes the Commission to bring civil action suits against nongovernmental respondents. Within a two-year period the Commission will assume responsibility for the general-pattern or practice suits now handled by the Justice Department. Court enforcement may become a far more effective mechanism for ameliorating employment discrimination.

Both the study by Nathan, *Jobs and Civil Rights*,[4] and the

[4] Richard P. Nathan, *Jobs and Civil Rights*, prepared for the U.S. Commission on Civil Rights by the Brookings Institution (Washington, D.C.: 1969).

review of Commission activities by the U.S. Commission on Civil Rights in its *Federal Civil Rights Enforcement Effort*[5] described the lengthy delays in the processing of complaints—up to almost two years—the enormous backlog of complaints, and the inadequate financial and staff resources. The Commission had been funded originally to handle an estimated 2,000 charges per year from complainants. During its first year, more than 8,000 charges were received, and in fiscal year 1971 approximately 29,000 complaints, over half alleging race discrimination, were handled. A substantial proportion of the conciliations had been unsuccessful (1,026 out of the 2,438 completed charges in 1971).[6] The fact that even the successful conciliations were not enforceable contracts made it difficult for the Commission to intervene effectively on behalf of persons who were discriminated against in labor markets.

The Commission's delivery system for EEO is linked to state and local fair-employment-practices commissions. The EEOC must defer processing of a complaint for at least a sixty-day period to state agencies with jurisdiction over the same types of discrimination and empowered to secure relief from such practices. Despite the fact that these agencies had enforcement powers, the fifth annual report of the Commission noted that over 85 percent of the complaints that have been deferred to state agencies for investigation ultimately were returned to the EEOC for handling. The deferral relationship with 35 states prolonged the period during which the complainant waited for redress, constrained federal efforts to modify or amend the investigation, and, more important, did not alleviate EEOC's enormous caseload.[7]

[5] U.S. Commission on Civil Rights, *Federal Civil Rights Enforcement Effort* (Washington, D.C.: Government Printing Office, 1970).

[6] U.S. Equal Employment Opportunity Commission, *Sixth Annual Report* (Washington, D.C.: Government Printing Office, 1972).

[7] See U.S. Equal Employment Opportunity Commission, *Fifth Annual Report* (Washington, D.C.: Government Printing Office, 1971).

Some of these deficiencies may have been partly offset by the affirmative enforcement programs that the Commission has established in partnership with state and local agencies. Section 709(b) of Title VII states that the Commission may reimburse state and local agencies charged with administration of state fair employment practices laws for services rendered to assist the Commission in carrying out this title. Here the emphasis is on broad efforts to attack systemic discrimination—those employment practices that have a disadvantageous effect on minorities and women even though the practices appear neutral on the surface. Over a million dollars was made available to state and local agencies to support these programs in 1971. The state and local FEP agencies are located mainly in the North and West.

The Civil Rights Commission study indicated that the EEOC had not developed broad enforcement mechanisms: class action suits had not been developed; priority had not been assigned to cases involving patterns of discrimination; too little use had been made of charges by EEOC Commissioners (in addition to those by aggrieved parties) to secure compliance in instances of pattern or industry-wide discrimination. Given the fact that such a large percentage of the EEOC's budget has been allocated to compliance activities, one then must examine other aspects of the process in order to determine whether effective means of equalizing employment and income outcomes for women and minority workers were developed.

The Broader Definition of Discrimination

At the time of the passage of Title VII, the operational definition of employment discrimination was restricted to a single, overt, and usually blatant act against an individual. As the Commission examined its minority employment data for public hearings on the textile industry in Charlotte, North Carolina, in January 1967, the pharmaceutical industry in October 1967, the white-collar hearings in New York City in January 1968, the utilities industry in Washington,

D.C., of June 1968, the Los Angeles hearing of March 1969, and the Houston hearings of June 1970, it became clear that the institutionalized patterns and procedures had unequal effect on employment outcomes.[8]

The ultimate sanction of Title VII has been judicial enforcement initiated by individual suits. Private litigants after they have exhausted state and federal procedures have brought hundreds of suits in the federal courts. Frequently the Commission was represented as a friend in court. After some delay, the Justice Department instituted general-pattern suits, but few such cases were referred by EEOC and even fewer filed by the Justice Department. Nevertheless, the body of case law being developed has contributed significantly to setting federal standards and clarifying the congressional intent.

The landmark decision on testing, the *Griggs* v. *Duke Power Company*,[9] may represent one of the most difficult policy issues growing out of the enactment of Title VII. Section 703(h), the Tower Amendment, had declared "nor shall it be an unlawful employment practice for an employer to give and to act upon the results of any professionally-developed ability test provided that such test, its administration, or action upon the results, is not designed, intended, or used to discriminate." The Commission's testing guidelines of August 1966 interpreted "professionally-developed ability test" to mean "a test which fairly measures the knowledge or skills required by the particular job or class

---

[8] See, for example, Phyllis A. Wallace and Maria Beckles, *1966 Employment Survey in the Textile Industry of the Carolinas*, Research Report 1966-11; Phyllis A. Wallace, *Employment Patterns in the Drug Industry*, 1966, Research Report 1967-20; Hearings Before the United States Equal Employment Opportunity Commission on *Discrimination in White Collar Employment*, New York, 1968; Hearings Before the United States Equal Employment Opportunity Commission on *Utilization of Minority and Women Workers in Certain Major Industries*, Los Angeles, 1969; and Hearings Before the United States Equal Employment Opportunity Commission on *Utilization of Minority and Women Workers in Certain Major Industries*, Houston, 1970.

[9] 401 U.S. 424 (1971).

of jobs which the applicant seeks, or which fairly affords the employer a chance to measure the applicant's ability to perform a particular job or class of jobs. The fact that a test was prepared by an individual or organization claiming expertise in test preparation does not, without more, justify its use within meaning of Title VII."[10]

In the *Griggs* case, the first occasion for the U.S. Supreme Court to rule on Title VII, black employees challenged the company's right to require a high school education or the passing of a standardized general intelligence test as a condition for employment, transfer, or promotion. The challenge was based on the fact that neither standard was shown to be related to job performance and that both requirements disqualified blacks at a substantially higher rate than whites. Justice Burger speaking for the Court stated in March 1971 that "The Equal Employment Opportunity Commission having enforcement responsibility has issued guidelines interpreting Section 703(h) to permit the use of job-related tests. The administrative interpretation of the Act by the enforcing agency is entitled to great deference. . . . Since the Act and its legislative history support the Commission's construction, this affords good reason to treat the guidelines as expressing the will of Congress."

The Supreme Court in *Griggs* states that practices, procedures, or tests neutral on their face and even neutral in intent, cannot be maintained if they operate to freeze the status quo of prior discriminatory employment practices. The heart of the *Griggs* decision in the statement of the Court is as follows: "What is required by the Congress is the removal of artificial, arbitrary, and unnecessary barriers to employment where the barriers operate invidiously to discriminate on the basis of racial or other impermissible classifications."

[10] U.S. Equal Employment Opportunity Commission, *Guidelines On Employment Testing Procedures*, August 24, 1966. See also *Guidelines on Employee Selection Procedures*, 35 F.R. 12333, August 1, 1970.

162

The *Griggs* decision is a major step toward the proper definition and identification of discrimination. Discriminatory practices and apparently neutral practices which perpetuate the effects of past discrimination are unlawful. In the long run, the decision will mean greater job opportunities for minority workers, with the impact being felt in union hiring halls and government offices as well as in private industry. Perhaps the adverse impact of other screening devices will be established.

After a thirty-year effort, the federal government has an employment opportunity agency equipped with court enforcement authority. An Equal Employment Opportunity Coordinating Council (EEOC, Secretary of Labor, Attorney General, Civil Service Commission, and Civil Rights Commission) has been established to develop and implement agreements, policies, and practices of federal agencies responsible for equal employment activities.

Sex Discrimination

Employment discrimination because of sex has now become an appropriate concern of the federal agencies responsible for equal employment opportunity. Although approximately one-fifth of all complaints filed with the EEOC have charged sex discrimination, mainly involving conditions and privileges of employment, initially the Commission did not move aggressively in this area.[11] There was considerable confusion over whether state protective laws regulating the employment of women were pre-empted by Title VII. Many states had enacted laws either limiting activities, such as working long hours or lifting heavy weights or conferring special benefits on women workers. In many instances the effects were not beneficial but restrictive of equal employment opportunities.

Categorization by sex where essential to the job may be regarded as a bona fide occupational qualification (BFOQ)

[11] Over a six-year period, 18,547 charges of employment discrimination because of sex out of 87,225 actionable charges.

163

under Title VII (Sec. 703[e]). A series of sex guidelines for compliance with Title VII were issued by the Commission between 1965 and 1969.[12] Previous policy statements were sometimes rescinded or reaffirmed until the August 1969 revisions declared that state laws limiting activities of women but not men were in conflict with Title VII, and were not a valid defense for an otherwise unlawful practice or a basis of a BFOQ exception. Even more stringent guidelines issued in April 1972 significantly broadened the scope of regulations against sex discrimination in employment as it related to recruitment, fringe benefits, maternity leaves, and wages. Interpretations of the law by the Commission in its decisions and published guidelines have been given "great deference" by the courts.[13]

The basic premise of Title VII is that individual workers must be judged as individuals and not on the basis of characteristics generally attributed to racial, religious, or sex groups. These are the so-called personal characteristics which are valued on the market. For example, it was only after a public hearing on the issue of whether sex was a bona fide occupational qualification for the position of flight attendants on airlines that the Commission ruled that the basic duties of a cabin attendant could be satisfactorily performed by members of both sexes.

The federal courts have thus far had a more important role in the evolution of the doctrine that capacities of women workers should be judged individually and not as a class. In four noteworthy decisions covering hours of work (*Mengelkoch* v. *California Industrial Welfare Commission*); maternity leave (*Schattman* v. *Texas Employment Commission*); weight lifting and hours of work (*Rosenfeld* v. *Southern Pacific Company*); and marital and family status (*Phillips* v. *Martin Marietta Corporation*) the courts have helped to shape a developing body of law on equal

[12] Title 29, Labor, Chapter XIV, Part 1604 of Code of Federal Regulations.

[13] See for example Griggs v. Duke Power Company.

participation in the economy for women.[14] To some extent the sex discrimination cases in the courts have been able to focus on substantive issues because of earlier procedural battles in the racial cases, particularly the fight to gain acceptance of the class action that allows relief for not only the named plaintiff but for those similarly situated.

4. OFFICE OF FEDERAL CONTRACT COMPLIANCE

The federal EEO delivery for the private sector has been weakened by the jurisdictional disputes, duplication of effort, lack of communication between federal agencies, and limited enforcement capability. The Office of Federal Contract Compliance of the Department of Labor (OFCC) has served mainly as a coordinator for federal contract compliance agencies. Although it is empowered to use strong sanctions (cancellation or termination of contract or debarment from further government contracts), these penalties have rarely been imposed. Considerable effort has been devoted to clarifying the concept of affirmative action.

Federal contractors were obliged under Executive Order No. 11246 to take "affirmative action" to assure that nondiscrimination in employment was achieved. Affirmative action included such activities as upgrading, transfer, recruitment, termination, compensation, and selection for training including apprenticeship. In May 1968 the requirement was established to develop a written plan of affirmative action with goals and timetables to correct deficiencies in equal employment opportunity. This requirement was amended in February 1970 by Order No. 4, which specified three basic obligations for nonconstruction federal contractors: (1) to analyze minority utilization in all job categories; (2) to establish goals and timetables to correct deficiencies,

---

[14] For further information see the following decisions: 473 F. 2d 563 (1971); 4 FEP Cases 353 (1972); 444 F. 2d 1219 (1971); and 400 U.S. 542 (1971).

and (3) to develop data collection systems and reporting plans documenting progress in achieving goals. Two and a half years passed before detailed standardized procedures were issued for complying with the regulation. Order 14 became effective as of July 1, 1972.[15]

Timetables, goals, and guidelines have also been established to achieve equal opportunity for minority groups in apprenticeship and training programs in the construction industry. Since 1967 the Urban League, the Workers Defense League, and the AFL-CIO have recruited minority youth and prepared them to pass examinations given by Joint Apprenticeship Committees. Approximately 12,000 minority youngsters have been placed in apprenticeship programs in the building and construction trades. Manpower training programs are now closely associated with metropolitan area plans developed to utilize more minority workers as skilled craftsmen on federally assisted construction projects. There are now about fifteen such training programs with the objective of securing full journeyman status for minorities in cities with "hometown plans."

The revised Philadelphia Plan and "hometown solutions" to expand employment opportunities for minorities in federally assisted construction contracts have perhaps generated more public controversy than any other aspect of the OFCC compliance program. In October 1971, four years after the original Philadelphia Plan was released, the Supreme Court upheld the legality of establishing goals and timetables on federally financed construction.[16] There is little assurance that the participants—unions, contractors, and minority community—in the fifty or so present plans will make a "good faith effort" to meet the goals set by the plans.

The limited success of the OFCC in improving minority

[15] The order covers contractors with 50 or more employees and $50,000 in contract funds.

[16] See Contractors of Eastern Pennsylvania v. Schultz, 311 F. Sub. 1002 (E.D. Pa., 1970), Appeal 3rd Circuit, 3 EPD8180.

166

employment patterns was associated with an attempt by a small staff to monitor and to implement an ambiguous concept of affirmative action. Essentially, affirmative action requires an aggressive stance, a willingness by contractors or construction unions to move beyond avoidance of overt discrimination. The attempt to make this objective operational has floundered. Procurement of goods and services rather than equal employment opportunity is seen as the primary objective of the contracting federal agencies. Even with the reduction of the number of compliance agencies from 26 to 15, emphasis on training programs for compliance officers, more sophisticated statistical measures, and increased budgets, the outcomes have been minimal.[17]

Efforts by OFCC to restrict sex discrimination lagged at least two years behind the application of executive orders, guidelines, and regulations to minority workers. Executive Order No. 11246 was signed in September 1965 and was amended to prohibit discrimination because of sex in October 1967. Order No. 4 requiring establishment of goals and timetables in affirmative action plans was not revised to include women until December 1971, almost two years after the original order was signed.

The affirmative action approach is not geared to redress the consequences of past discrimination. Hearings held on the proposed debarment of the Bethlehem Steel facility at Sparrows Point, Maryland, demonstrated the difficulties of alleviating the continuing effects of past discrimination against minority workers.[18] The courts have dealt with this issue in the seniority cases and have ruled that "It is apparent that Congress did not intend to freeze an entire generation of Negro employees into discriminatory patterns that existed before the Act."[19]

[17] See criticism of OFCC performance in *Equal Employment Opportunities Enforcement Act of 1971*, Senate Report No. 92-415, 92nd Cong., 1st Session.
[18] OFCC Docket No. 102-68.
[19] Quarles v. Philip Morris, Inc., 297 F. Supp. 505 (E.D., Va., 1968).

5. U.S. CIVIL SERVICE COMMISSION

The model provided by the U.S. Government in its role as civilian employer is one where minorities and women are over-represented in the least desirable jobs. In 1970, minority workers constituted 19.4 percent of the full-time federal civilian work force but were mainly concentrated in the lower-income brackets for each pay system.[20] Women held only about 5 percent of all executive positions (GS 12 and above) in the federal government.[21] Since employees and applicants for employment may now file civil action suits under provisions of the Equal Employment Act of 1972, it is likely that equal employment opportunity may become more fully and effectively integrated into the personnel programs of the federal government.

The Commission could set standards which state and local governments might emulate. About ten million employees from these governments have for the first time been brought under Title VII of the Civil Rights Act of 1964 as amended by the Equal Employment Act of 1972. A 1969 report by the U.S. Civil Rights Commission examined equal opportunity in state and local government employment and concluded "Not only do state and local governments consciously and overtly discriminate in hiring and promoting minority group members, but they do not foster positive programs to deal with discriminatory treatment on the job."[22]

[20] U.S. Civil Service Commission, *Study of Minority Group Employment in the Federal Government* (Washington, D.C.: Government Printing Office, 1970).

[21] U.S. Civil Service Commission, *Study of Employment of Women in the Federal Government* (Washington, D.C.: Government Printing Office, 1969).

[22] U.S. Commission on Civil Rights, *For All the People, By All The People* (Washington, D.C.: Government Printing Office, 1969), p. 131.

6. PROGRESS SINCE 1965

Assessment of the federal equal employment opportunity activity since 1965 reveals how difficult it is for small agencies with limited resources to deal effectively with powerful coalitions of employers, unions, bureaucrats, congressmen, and others. As racial and other tensions have intensified and have fragmented the civil rights-labor-liberal coalition of the sixties, the processes of translating equal employment opportunity into public policy have become bogged down. Many elements in the minority community appear to have opted for more direct tactics. Certainly the greater ethnic cohesion, the impact of community action programs and the emphasis on community control, participatory democracy, and activism have undermined some of the assumptions of the legal-gradualism approaches to equal opportunity. Programs emphasizing education and moral suasion are perceived as fraudulent.

From the social science literature, we know that, experimentally at least, induced behavior change that runs counter to one's attitudes may be one of the strongest motives for producing attitudinal change. Such a change brings attitudes in line with the way in which one is already acting. This model emphasizes action with attitudinal change as a consequence of behavioral change. In this case, when one's behavior is no longer consistent with one's attitudes, the latter are changed to be in line with one's new actions.[23]

The prospects for significant gains in the short run are bleak. Even with the expansion of supportive programs in manpower development and training, and of court enforcement, the federal EEO delivery system that has evolved is cumbersome, ad hoc, and not nearly so comprehensive as

[23] Based on work by Festinger and students as noted in Norman M. Bradburn et al., *Racial Integration in American Neighborhoods* (Chicago: National Opinion Research Center, 1970), p. 209.

it could be. For example, since 1967 the EEOC has collected apprenticeship information (EEOC-2) from joint labor-management apprenticeship committees and referral (hiring hall) union data (EEO-3), and it did not validate these statistics against data collected by the Labor Department or other sources until 1971-1972.[24] It is presumed that the AFL-CIO headquarters had its own data bank. Cross-checking and earlier validation would have been beneficial to all parties. However, the program priorities for government and labor have focused on other matters. I anticipate a more positive role for trade unions in helping to advance the economic status of minorities through achievement of equal employment opportunity.[25]

7. ALTERNATIVE STRATEGIES

Before we can design more effective techniques of achieving equal employment opportunity, we need to raise serious questions about present institutions, policies, and procedures.

Litigation

Why should the person who suffers the discrimination bear so much of the costs of litigation? The time, energy, and persistence needed for lengthy litigation and the harassment and other psychological burdens it may impose are rarely publicized. Some of the private litigation has been handled by civil rights and other legal agencies on behalf of the aggrieved individual. In 1969 the Chairman of the EEOC noted that court action had been initiated in less

[24] See, for example, Herbert Hammerman, "Minority Workers in Construction Referral Unions," *Monthly Labor Review*, 94 (May 1971), 17-26.

[25] See Phyllis A. Wallace, "Economic Position and Prospects for Urban Blacks," *American Journal of Agricultural Economics*, 53 (May 1971), 316-318.

than 10 percent of those cases in which conciliation attempts were not successful.

Admittedly, class action suits may produce benefits to a group within the same department, plant, firm, industry, etc. The restrictive Erlenborn bill on equal employment opportunity, which was passed by the House in September 1971, eliminated the right of an employee to bring a class action suit on behalf of other employees similarly situated; limited back pay to no more than two years (in the 1972 Act); and made Title VII the exclusive federal remedy for relief from discriminatory employment practices.

Since only a few patterns-of-discrimination suits have been filed by the Justice Department, ways must be found to reduce the costs of litigation. An amendment of Title VII to eliminate the confidentiality provisions might produce results. The Commission conducts an annual survey of employment of minorities and women, and also collects information on referral unions and apprenticeship programs. If the minority employment data for some of the largest companies and unions were made available to the public, such organizations might be induced to alter their employment practices. Because it is highly visible, the construction industry has received perhaps more than its share of unfavorable publicity. Whether it is the World Trade Center or a construction site within an urban renewal area, workers can be identified. It is more difficult to undertake a visual survey of a chemical plant, an automobile factory, or an airlines facility.

A Federal Model

How can the U.S. civilian government set equal employment objectives without being a model employer itself? Impediments to equal employment opportunity have developed in the federal civil service system. Last year a federal hearing examiner found the Department of Housing and Urban Development guilty of racial discrimination and stated that, at least prior to October 1970, a pattern of discrimination existed in the Department's employment practices.[26]

Serious questions have been raised about the validation of tests used by the U.S. Civil Service Commission to determine entry into managerial and professional jobs in the federal service (*Douglass* v. *Hampton*).[27] These concerns deal with whether the Commission's methods of determining job relatedness are consonant with accepted procedures in industrial psychology. More importantly, standards enunciated by the Supreme Court in the *Griggs* case should be met by the federal government in its role as civilian employer.

Retention of Staff

Can the present machinery for settling grievances be improved? A cadre of attorneys skilled in Title VII litigation is slowly being trained. It has been a general practice for bright young lawyers to join federal regulatory agencies, train on the job, and then leave for more lucrative positions with the regulated constituency. Attorneys who have worked for one of the federal equal employment agencies may have fewer options.

NLRB Involvement

The National Labor Relations Board has not been an active participant in the federal EEO delivery system, and, with its emphasis on collective bargaining, it may prefer not to serve as an advocate for women and minority workers. However, a recent decision under the National Labor Relations Act (*United Packinghouse Union* v. *NLRB*) found discrimination by an employer to be in violation of the act.[28] One labor relations expert, Jones, has suggested that dis-

[26] See Paul Delaney, "HUD Is Charged With Racial Bias," *New York Times*, October 23, 1971, p. 11.
[27] 4 FEP Cases 32; F Supp., D.D.C. (1972).
[28] 396 U.S. 903 (1969).

establishment of labor unions that discriminate might provide a more effective equal employment remedy than those now in use. The NLRB has the authority to disestablish a union (withdraw its recognition as the representative of employees for the purpose of dealing with grievances, labor disputes, wages, hours, and other conditions of employment). Although Jones states that "there is no substantial impediment under the fair labor practices provision of the NLRB barring the proposed remedy of disestablishment" in racial discrimination cases, "prudence suggests that the quest for the disestablishment remedy be pursued directly in the courts, as well as before the Board." The remedy should be imposed only in egregious cases of discrimination by unions.[29]

Patterns of Discrimination

If the EEOC could set a one-year moratorium on the processing of individual complaints and spend 90 percent of its budget on industry-wide pattern approaches and other technical assistance programs, this would be a great improvement over the present efforts. The concept of multidefendant suits might be developed under its court enforcement procedures. One of the most creative examples of investigating system-wide sex and race discrimination hearings has been the materials prepared by the EEOC for its hearings on the Bell System (AT&T), the largest private employer in the country. The Commission filed a complaint with the Federal Communications Commission charging employment discrimination by the company.[30]

Minority Advancement Plan

Recently, the Galbraith/Kuh/Thurow Plan for Minority Advancement (MAP) was published in the *New York*

[29] See, for example, James E. Jones, "Disestablishing of Labor Unions For Engaging In Racial Discrimination—A New Use For An Old Remedy," *Wisconsin Law Review*, Vol. 1972, No. 2, pp. 373-376.

[30] See Lydon Christopher, "Job Bias at Bell Charged by Panel," *New York Times*, December 2, 1971, p. 1.

Times. MAP emphasizes movement into jobs in the middle- and upper-level positions. Galbraith and partners suggest a ten-year period mainly for large firms (over 2,000 employees), the federal government, and educational institutions to recruit, train, and promote women and minority workers to middle- and upper-level positions in accord with the representation of these groups in the labor force of the community. Penalties would be set for failure to meet requirements and incentives given (in the form of educational grants) for state and local governments to join.[31] If it appears that a quota system can be set for jobs with status, power, and money, this might be sufficient to induce other employers to comply with the weaker provisions of Title VII. Quotas are presently prohibited under Title VII.

State and Local Funding

Why not allocate an additional billion dollars under the special revenue-sharing proposal to strengthen and enhance equal employment opportunity? If sufficient funds were available to state and local governments to undertake legitimate and serious activities on equal opportunity, one might expect these commissions to achieve meaningful enforcement within rigorous federal guidelines on equal employment opportunity.

Centralized EEO Agency

A single federal EEO agency might best provide the means for achieving equal employment opportunity. Of course, there are the great risks of centralizing such controversial functions in one agency, for it would surely not receive adequate appropriations. Under the present diffusion of responsibility, EEO activities require only a small part of large departmental budgets and, when political and other pressures are applied, the Secretaries and other high-

[31] See, for example, John K. Galbraith et al., "The Galbraith Plan to Promote Minorities," *New York Times Magazine*, August 22, 1971, p. 9.

level appointees are held accountable. Yet it is clear that the greatest potential for improving the relative income position of minorities and women through the federal EEO delivery system would be by establishing a unified, comprehensive attack on the different kinds of discrimination.[32] The entire staff of such an agency would receive specialized training, depending on need, in both government and nongovernment facilities. The federal government pays roughly $53,000 to educate a young man at the Air Force Academy. It should be willing to pay less to train and develop an elite corps of specialists on some of the problems we have itemized.

Multiple Minorities

As long as some Americans perceive a civil rights agency to be predominantly black-oriented, it will receive only minimal support. Minorities, however they are categorized, can make gains only if other groups in the society do not feel threatened. Thus, such an agency could serve as an advocate for the many racial, ethnic, and other subgroups in a pluralistic society. It might well be designated as "The Commission on American Affairs." As certain minimum objectives are attained, it should be guaranteed that this special agency to redress old grievances and to equalize a variety of outcomes would be phased out.

These policy considerations of equal employment opportunity have been examined mainly for a period of high level of economic activity (such as 1965-1969). Different priorities might be established in a slack economy. Certainly the current controversy over the dual labor market hypothesis and the inflation/unemployment dilemma complicates any discussion of the impact of equal employment opportunity programs.

[32] *Equal Employment Opportunities Enforcement Act of 1971*, p. 139.

Dale L. Hiestand   COMMENT

Dr. Wallace has provided an excellent elucidation of the present system of federal policies and programs to deal with employment discrimination. I will confine my remarks to three points: the economic preconditions for an effective anti-discrimination program, the conflict between individualistic and class-based concepts of discrimination, and priorities in program efforts.

The first point to be made is that efforts to promote equal employment opportunity stand little chance of being effective as long as unemployment levels for the total labor force continue to be high. My own studies and recent experience demonstrate that the occupational and income positions of minorities improves significantly relative to whites only in periods of very full employment, i.e. World War II, the Korean War, and during the early years of the Vietnam War.[1] In the absence of a buoyant job market, there are fewer opportunities for new hires and promotions, and majority group workers fight for and tend to win those which become available.

Policies to produce full employment are thus the primary instrument to secure more equal employment, and their success is a necessary condition for the effective operation of machinery specifically set up for that purpose. Indeed, a significant reduction in the level of unemployment among minority groups would make a larger contribution to their welfare than would any change in their relative occupation-

[1] Dale L. Hiestand, *Economic Growth and Employment Opportunities for Minorities* (New York: Columbia University Press, 1964); U.S. Dept. of Labor, Bureau of Labor Statistics, *The Negroes in the United States: Their Economic and Social Situation*, Bulletin No. 1511, p. 138, and *Black Americans: A Chartbook*, Bulletin No. 1699, p. 38.

al position which might conceivably occur over a period of several years.

Second, it may be necessary to recognize explicitly the "class" nature of discrimination, and thus raise more clearly the issue of "class" remedies. Sometimes Dr. Wallace discusses discrimination as something affecting a group, i.e. a class phenomenon, but the emphasis on "equal opportunity" connotes a problem in individual opportunity.

I would submit that the basic concept of a labor market used by most economists is atomistic in nature. Thus, the problem is conceived of as one of individual opportunity. Given this implicit view, it is little wonder that the public and the Congress conceptualize the problem as one to be remedied through legal processes initiated by individuals. Dr. Wallace rightly points out that most analysts have concluded that such an approach has little effect.

Dr. Wallace equates employment discrimination with "differential valuation of labor input of equal productivity." The problem is that in a modern society it becomes increasingly difficult to measure or predict productivity.

For this and other reasons, jobs are to a large and increasing extent socially, not atomistically, allocated. Large sectors of the labor market—both external and internal to business and nonprofit employers—are controlled by various social mechanisms, usually in the name of equity. Thus these mechanisms have a wide measure of social support. They effectively determine which kinds of individuals get which jobs in the system.

The mechanisms for the social allocation of jobs are diverse. Trade unions control large segments of the job market for their members. Referral unions—the present legal transmogrification of the old "closed" shop—fairly effectively limit jobs in the unionized parts of the skilled construction and some other trades to their members. The existing union members also exercise considerable control over who becomes a new member. Ordinarily, new members are relatives and friends of old members, with only limited attention to predictions of productivity. Individual productivity has little meaning in any case, for output is controlled implicitly or explicitly by work rules or custom. The social allocation of jobs by referral unions clearly enjoys a strong legal position and great political and social support.

In other large sectors, jobs are also allocated by social mechanisms other than individual employer-employee contracts. One simple device for the social allocation of civil service jobs is veterans preference. Another popular device in many large industrial, commercial, and service organizations is that of promoting from within. Where this is the rule, jobs above the entry level effectively belong to the present employees, whether by union contract or custom. Promotion on the basis of seniority, save for demonstrated inability, developed as a method of equitably allocating a great range of blue collar, white collar, and even many managerial jobs—hence the Peter Principle. The age progression thus built into most large organizations is a highly approved method of socially allocating jobs and incomes.

In this light, the use of educational standards, hiring tests, professional licenses, and the like can also be seen as devices for socially approved allocations of jobs and income. Employers utilize devices such as education and test scores as indices of potential productivity. These assumptions are rarely tested or testable. Indeed, in large bureaucracies, individual productivity again has little meaning, for the rate of production is socially determined, as in the case of class size rules agreed upon by teachers' organizations and school boards.

Unfortunately, the assumptions that education and test scores measure productivity often get written into legislation, professional standards, merit systems, and the like. They then become the instruments for the allocation of jobs and promotion. Hence the significance of the *Griggs* v. *Duke* decision, leaving standing the EEOC guidelines requiring tests and educational criteria to be validated against performance if they are to be used.

Many personnel executives have long realized the shaky grounds on which such educational and test standards often stand as devices to select the most productive employees. However, with a surfeit of applicants, such methods provide a convenient device to limit the field by raising educational qualifications, and finally settling on individuals with relatively high test scores. Whatever the hiring officer thought he was doing, his method had the approval of all but the most sophisticated. Executives, workers, applicants, and the public all considered such actions to be only "good common sense."[2]

I am not arguing that educational standards, the merit system, and the like are necessarily invalid. However, they are very often systems for the social allocation of jobs and have little to do with productivity. Under them, people are given priority in obtaining jobs if they have social advantages and conform closely to socially defined behavioral norms: that is, they come from "advantaged" families which inculcate certain forms of behavior approved by their in-group, including continuation in school regardless of content until certain credentials are gained, docilely taking tests however irrelevant they may be, and the like.

What happens when such decision crutches are no longer permissible? Employers are in a most unenviable position if they have too many applicants and no socially and legally approved decision system for the allocation of jobs. Inevitably, the decision to hire becomes a kind of lottery. Personnel officials know they are making arbitrary decisions, with

[2] For comments on the use of hiring standards to narrow the field, and their relaxation in tight labor markets, see Albert Rees, "Information Networks in Labor Markets," *American Economic Review*, 56, No. 2 (May 1966), pp. 561-562; for evidence on the variability and subjectivity of hiring standards and their questionable relationship to job performance, see Hrach Bedosian and Daniel E. Diamond, *Hiring Standards and Job Performance*, U.S. Department of Labor, Manpower Administration, 1970, Manpower Research Monograph No. 18, pp. 1-6; see also Ivar Berg, *Education and Jobs: The Great Training Robbery* (New York: Praeger, 1970), esp. Ch. V.

little logic to support them. In such a case, goals set in affirmative action programs may become a source of comfort. They represent a legally approved decision instrument when none other is available. Thus, "goals" may be converted into realities, i.e. they become "quotas."

But are such "goals" socially approved? This is the nub of the matter. The crucial question seems to be whether legitimacy will develop for a system of socially allocating jobs on the basis of belonging to a group (i.e. a race, minority group, or sex) which is subject to unfavorable discrimination. We already have widespread social approval for mechanisms which do tend to discriminate in favor of certain groups on the basis of race or sex, such as whites and men. The new mechanisms, "goals," for socially allocating jobs would tend to counterbalance existing mechanisms which work to the detriment of blacks, Puerto Ricans, Mexican-Americans, women, etc.

My final observations on priorities in equal employment programs are directly related to the two previous points. The evidence suggests that discrimination against minority groups and women is stronger in the managerial, sales, skilled, and professional occupations, as well as in clerical occupations for male minority workers.

By all indications, future job growth will probably be in these occupations in the service and governmental sectors, rather than in the blue collar and manufacturing sectors. These fields, therefore, would seem to deserve priority in planning equal employment actions.

These are the fields, however, in which productivity is most difficult to measure, much less to predict. Indeed, given social controls on the rate of production, individual productivity often has little meaning in these fields. In all of them, moreover, educational and testing criteria and "merit" systems have been widespread, in large part, I would suggest, precisely because it is so difficult to evaluate productivity in them.

180

Clearly, these fields will be the center of controversy for the foreseeable future. It therefore behooves analysts to develop the concepts, techniques, and perhaps the rhetoric which will contribute to the resolution of these foreseeable conflicts.

Library of Congress Cataloging in Publication Data

Conference on Discrimination in Labor Markets,
    Princeton University, 1971.
    Discrimination in labor markets.

    1. Discrimination in employment—United States—
Congresses. I. Ashenfelter, Orley, 1942-   ed.
II. Rees, Albert, 1921-   ed. III. Princeton University.
IV. Title.
HD4903.5.U58C63   1971   331.1'33'0973   72-4037
ISBN 0-691-04170-9